Build Your Confidence with CBT

About the author

Manja de Neef is a cognitive behavioural therapist based in Amsterdam. She has worked for over thirty years for various mental health institutions with various client populations, including an academic anxiety polyclinic. She specializes in the treatment of low self-esteem of clients with serious anxiety or mood problems. Manja is a teacher and supervisor at the Dutch Association of Behavioural and Cognitive Therapy and is associated with a training institute for post-academic education in Amsterdam. She has written self-help books about low self-esteem, compulsion and phobias, and devised an e-health programme for enhancing low self-esteem.

Build Your Confidence with CBT

6 simple steps to be happier, more successful, and fulfilled

Manja de Neef

Open University Press
McGraw-Hill Education
McGraw-Hill House
Shoppenhangers Road
Maidenhead
Berkshire
England
SL6 2QL

email: enquiries@openup.co.uk
world wide web: www.openup.co.uk

and Two Penn Plaza, New York, NY 10121-2289, USA

A catalogue record of this book is available from the British Library

ISBN-13: 978-0-33-526224-3
ISBN-10: 0-33-526224-4
eISBN: 978-0-33-526225-2

Library of Congress Cataloging-in-Publication Data
CIP data applied for

Typeset by Transforma Pvt. Ltd., Chennai, India

Printed by Bell and Bain Ltd, Glasgow

MIX
Paper from
responsible sources
FSC
www.fsc.org   FSC® C007785

Contents

7 Dealing with Criticism

8 High Demands and Perfectionism

9 The Future

1
Introduction

Michael is a handsome guy with blonde curly hair and brown eyes. He is tall, lean, sporty, easy-going and empathetic. You would think there is nothing wrong with him but on the inside, he feels very different. He does not think much of himself, and believes that he will fall short and that people will find out he's a 'nobody'. He fears that his good looks are nothing more than an empty shell. He has low self-esteem, which is becoming a bit of a concern.

Why this book?

There are many people who, like Michael, suffer from low self-esteem. They think of themselves as a failure, that they are stupid or that they do not fit in – this combines with negative emotions such as sadness and fear. Some will experience a continuous feeling of worthlessness, whereas for others it lurks in the background, arising in daily life when, for example, they stumble in public, they lose their car keys or when a friend does not contact them for a week. Things begin to worsen after such a setback and so they conclude: 'This proves it, I am a failure!' or 'I knew I didn't fit in'. They do the same when someone criticizes them, which is why criticism feels like a stab in the back. They are also more emotional in the way they react than one would expect. Their low self-esteem manifests itself in the way they look at and talk about themselves. For example, they often highlight the things they have got wrong, and undervalue and judge themselves constantly. They have a pessimistic view of the future and expect little success.

People with low self-esteem develop strategies to avoid confronting negative feelings about themselves. They may retreat into themselves or avoid contact with other people, and may play it safe in their relationships, in education or at work. This is yet another reason why they judge themselves. The opposite can also occur, as some individuals may become over-active instead.

To ensure they cannot be faulted, they spend inordinate amounts of time working on tasks, such as preparing a presentation for work, and feel compelled to offer help to others, even if this greatly inconveniences them. And even then, they are rarely satisfied.

> 'Am I suited to nursing?', Agnieszka asks her tutor. 'Shouldn't I pick another profession?' In the second year of her nursing training, Agnieszka is working as an intern in the department of internal medicine of a large hospital. She has no trouble whatsoever with the theory and she can study for hours on end. But the practical subjects take a lot of effort and she is worried stiff, especially now that she has to work with people. She feels insecure about everything she does and is scared that she might miss things or make mistakes. When helping patients, she thinks that she says the wrong thing and is terrified of an unfavourable assessment. Working with patients does not give her any joy and she has little contact with colleagues. She is tense all the time and, as a consequence, often goes home with a headache.
>
> Agnieszka is sombre and refrains from contact with others but that is nothing new, as she has suffered from similar feelings before. She believes that she just needs to study more and it will pass, so she dives into her books and studies each evening. She does not answer the phone or respond when her roommate knocks on the door. She thinks that others consider her odd and feels like an outsider in her student accommodation, resulting in a feeling of not fitting in.

Low self-esteem is the result of a strong negative conviction about oneself that manifests itself in people's thinking, feelings and behaviour. It influences and restricts many parts of their lives and rarely disappears by itself.

How do you overcome low self-esteem and improve your confidence?

The approach described in this book is based on Cognitive Behavioural Therapy (CBT). The basic presumption of CBT is that problems emerge once normal daily events are repeatedly perceived from a negative point of view, caused by a negative conviction about yourself, in CBT called 'negative core belief'. As a consequence, you experience negative feelings which you may try to deal with by developing behaviour which is actually dysfunctional rather than helpful.

CBT focuses on influencing your negative core belief by changing your dysfunctional views and behaviours. In doing so, your feelings, self-esteem, and confidence will automatically change too.

It is not easy to turn a negative core belief into something positive when you have carried it with you for many years. Over time, you will have started believing in your negative conviction and begun behaving accordingly. Its roots run deep.

1

Steve (36, divorced with twin daughters, Marie and Chris) came close to graduating. He studied political science and he did okay. However, he was sure that he would never be able to handle a university-level job and ended up working in the catering industry before working as a freelance editor for the staff magazine. When he was offered permanent employment, he was scared off so left the company and worked as a bus driver for a while, then a tour guide and had many other short-term jobs. 'Jack-of-all-trades and master of none', he mocked himself.

When the twins were born, Steve applied for a job at a publisher of schoolbooks. Later, he worked at a housing corporation and as a supply teacher of social studies. Finding a new job was never a problem for Steve, but as soon as he found new work, the doubts began. He always thought: 'They don't know what they have let themselves in for.' Two months ago, he started training as a primary school teacher and was allowed to teach in front of a class right away due to his previous experience. He himself has to attend classes one day a week. The interview was a piece of cake, but Steve wonders how long he will be able to keep things up this time around.

It takes time, but if you go about it systematically, you can grow in confidence and boost your self-esteem. Changing your negative view of yourself means that you start paying more attention to what goes right, instead of solely focusing on what goes wrong. You will learn to do this in Chapter 3, and in Chapters 4 and 5 you will learn to do so even better. Once you start paying more attention to positive events in your life and put negative events to the back of your mind, you will start feeling better and more positive about yourself.

To change your behaviour, you need to replace the behaviour patterns that go with your negative view of yourself with behaviours associated with a new positive core belief. Even though the changes you make will be small, if you change your behaviour you will notice other (positive) experiences. This in turn will help you to realize you can influence your own life and your self-esteem and confidence will grow – this is covered in Chapters 6, 7, and 8.

The final chapter is about the future – how to continue what you have learned and what to do to develop even more confidence. And how to deal with possible relapse.

Denise has a contagious laugh that can often be heard in the schoolyard when she is playing with the kids. You can also hear it when she talks to other mums who supervise the playground. 'It is nervous laughter,' she says. 'In fact, I'm not a very happy person. I always feel like I'm a failure and then I panic.' At school, she is quite at ease now because she has been there a long time. Her eldest son Murat is ten, Elmas is eight, and her youngest daughter Olgun is at nursery. Denise has been a playground supervisor for a year now, ever since her neighbour, Gizem, dragged her along. Denise would not have considered it without Gizem's encouragement, though she has begun to wonder whether she should continue. She is always exhausted at the end of her shift and feels sad that she cannot join in as much as the other helpers because she is conscious of her nervous laugh. She would like to do more at school, in the PTA for instance, by decorating the school for seasonal events or making costumes for the school musical. They are always on the lookout for people that can help out, but she is afraid to apply.

Who is this book for?

1 This book is written for people who, just like Michael, Agnieszka, Steve, and Denise, think badly about themselves – people who feel they are worthless and don't fit in. It is for people who are constantly stressed or who may have become depressed because of the restrictions imposed by their low self-esteem. This book is for people who want to change how they feel about themselves, and are willing to put in the effort needed to make that change.

How does this self-help programme work?

Research has shown that self-help really does work. Self-help means that you take responsibility for your own problems. With a self-help programme, just as in therapy, you are given homework exercises to do – but without the help of a therapist or a coach.

There are advantages and disadvantages to self-help. One advantage is that you can decide on your own when and at what pace you will undertake the exercises. One disadvantage is that there is no expert in the background, although therapeutic instructions can easily be portrayed on paper, as they are here. A therapist thinks along with you, supports you, and helps you through tough times. They will praise you when you take difficult steps and encourage you when your attention slips. They will maintain a steady pace so that you do not easily give up. Custom-made support is nigh impossible to provide in a book, but the tips provided here should help you when problems arise during your self-help journey. You will also find examples of people who have struggled with the same problems as you and by reading their stories you will better understand how to put the advice offered into practice.

Self-help is based on the premise that you will be highly motivated and complete your exercises on a regular basis. This means you should undertake the exercises seriously and attentively, even when you are not feeling so good.

A matter of motivation ...

Building your self-esteem and confidence requires perseverance. You have to work hard at it to see results. To change your negative point of view and behaviour, you first have to be aware of the problem and its consequences, although this may not be enough to motivate you to change. Saying goodbye to the negative feelings about yourself can be a relief, but letting go can also make you feel uncomfortable or uneasy. You should become aware of how your low self-esteem affects you, but also of any advantages there have been. In Exercise 1.1, you will describe these advantages and disadvantages in a so-called 'cost–benefit analysis'. Furthermore, it is useful for you to visualize what you can gain from the self-help programme. Imagine something really concrete, as it will help you realize why it is worth the effort. The disadvantages of change are also discussed because they can be inhibiting factors. In Exercise 1.2, you will address the advantages and disadvantages of living with a new positive view of yourself – it is important that you feel the advantages outweigh the disadvantages (or costs) of change (see Exercise 1.3).

This self-help programme will take about six months, but you will notice its effects much earlier than that. When, after a little while, you can think more positively about yourself, you will experience feelings of contentment, joy, even pride. This will motivate you further, but do not be surprised if your motivation diminishes every now and then. You may not always feel like working on your exercises or you may lack the energy to do so. Change, however, usually occurs in stages: you work on it for a while, you achieve something, and then you stop for a bit. And then you start on the next stage, take a step forward, and let it rest again. This is normal and you will find a work rate that suits you.

At first, Steve mainly sees the disadvantages of thinking positively about himself. He thinks he will become lazy and less caring or that maybe he will overdo it and become insufferable. But then he remembers his ex-wife, Helen, who is not held back by self-doubt. He used to be jealous of that – she is relaxed, stable, and deals easily with stress. These are the advantages that he can clearly see.

Picking the right moment

Although you choose the pace at which to work, a self-help programme requires dedication. You should not just read the book, but do the exercises as well. This takes time and requires your attention. Ensure nothing is likely to stand in your way before you start.

* *Do you experience feelings of depression?* Low self-esteem makes you vulnerable and often goes hand in hand with low mood. If you are depressed, you may not have the energy to work on a self-help programme and it would therefore be better to seek professional help. However, if you are just feeling gloomy

because of your low self-esteem, then this book can definitely help you.

- *Do you suffer from anxiety issues or do you have other problems, such as an eating disorder, an addiction or aggressive tendencies?* If your low self-esteem is caused by problems such as these and you have a positive view of yourself in other respects, you should address the anxiety issues or other disorders first. Successful treatment of these problems will likely enhance your self-esteem. If your negative core belief influences your entire existence, it is useful to work on that conviction and also seek help for your other problems.
- *Are you likely to be distracted by other things?* Do you have to take care of a family member or help your dyslexic child with their homework? If there are other worries or practical problems to deal with, there will be little room for working on a self-help programme and it is best to resolve any other issues before embarking on one.
- *Are there other things going on that demand your attention?*
  It is not just problems that can distract you from your work – happy occasions can do so as well! Marriage, pregnancy, changing your job, moving house, each will demand a lot of your attention.
  You yourself are best qualified to decide whether you are able to follow this self-help programme in addition to your other commitments.

How to use this book

Although there is no quick fix to raise your self-esteem and become more confident, the exercises should only take about half an hour a day. You do not have to progress quickly through the programme but it is important that you focus. The changes you make do not have to be huge, as small changes have a positive effect too. To gain an impression of what is in store, you could first leaf through the book and read a bit here and there, or select an exercise to look at.

You will find the chapters have a similar format. After an overview of what is to follow and some background information, stories are provided of people who also have experienced low self-esteem. You will then be required to do a couple of exercises; you will be guided on how much time to allow and what steps you need to take.

Seeking help from a buddy

Research shows that self-help combined with therapy or coaching is better than self-help alone. You remember positive events better when you relate them to others and this will increase the likelihood of you persevering with the programme. Coaching does not have to be done by a professional and does not need to be intensive. A regular short phone call should suffice, and it is worth asking someone you know to act as your buddy for this project (see Exercise 1.4) – they will likely be pleased to have been asked and enthusiastic to help. You can let them read the book or tell them about its contents.

1

Exercises

Exercise 1.1: Advantages and disadvantages of low self-esteem

Changing your negative view of yourself begins by becoming aware
of the disadvantages of low self-esteem and how it hinders you.
Consider also any advantages of low self-esteem, these will hold you
back if you really want to change.

- *Time to allow: 30 minutes*
- *How to go about it*

   ✓ List the advantages and disadvantages of your low self-
     esteem.

Cost–benefit analysis of my low self-esteem

Advantages	Disadvantages

Exercise 1.2: Advantages and disadvantages of a positive view of oneself

Thinking of how your life will improve based on a new positive core
belief will provide a real boost. Not wanting to change, or feeling
unable to change, is often the result, subconsciously, of being afraid
of the effects of thinking positively about yourself.

- *Time to allow: 30 minutes*
- *How to go about it*

   ✓ List the advantages and disadvantages of living with a new
     positive core belief.

Cost–benefit analysis of living with a new positive core belief

Advantages	Disadvantages

Exercise 1.3: Am I sufficiently motivated?

Compare the two cost–benefit analyses and decide what is most important to you. If you see more advantages in changing, then the time is ripe to start the self-help programme. If the disadvantages outweigh the advantages, your efforts will have little effect. Your time will be better spent trying to discover more advantages of living with a positive view of yourself.

* *Time to allow: 30 minutes*
* *How to go about it*

  ✓ Look at the two cost–benefit analyses from the previous exercises once again.
  ✓ Become truly aware of all advantages and disadvantages.
  ✓ Draw a conclusion from this information and write down your intentions.

My motivation

My conclusion after considering the advantages and disadvantages is as follows:

....

I intend to:

....

Exercise 1.4: Do I want to involve a buddy?

It is quite something to change your behaviour and the way you look at yourself. It is nice to ask someone to help you with this process and if you think about what to ask your buddy beforehand, you can maintain control of the situation.

- *Time to allow: 30 minutes*
- *How to go about it*

  - ✓ Decide whether you want to involve a buddy and who you would like it to be.
  - ✓ Ask your buddy to help you and explain to them what you want to do.
  - ✓ Let them read the information in this book.

A buddy

I want to involve a buddy: yes/no

I would like as my buddy:

....

Mark below what you want to ask your buddy:

- ✓ Help plan my exercises.
- ✓ Do exercises with me.
- ✓ Support and encourage me.
- ✓ Praise me when I have completed an exercise.
- ✓ Help me through tough periods.
- ✓ ....
- ✓ ....

Advice for your buddy

It is great that you want to support your partner, friend or family member. For people who wish to improve their confidence, a buddy can be a great support and the advice below should be helpful to you.

- *What you should do*

  ✓ Support your partner/friend/family member without judging or condemning them.
  ✓ Encourage and praise them.
  ✓ Show them understanding and warmth and be available.
  ✓ It would be helpful to read the information in this book, so you know what the programme is about and what you can do to help.
  ✓ It is a good thing if your partner/friend/family member is in control.
  ✓ Do not exert too much pressure and do not take control – this will have an adverse effect. But do not be overprotective either. If you persevere, your partner/friend/family member will be encouraged by this and will also persevere.
  ✓ What you will be required to do exactly will depend on the wishes and instructions of your partner/friend/family member, which can change over time. Ask them to be as clear as possible what is expected of you.

- *What you shouldn't do*

  ✓ Criticize your partner/friend/family member. Criticism results in even more insecurity.
  ✓ Exert too much pressure when your partner/friend/family member is not yet ready for it.
  ✓ Give up. Remember, it takes time to overcome low self-esteem – but it is definitely worth persevering!

2
Your
self-esteem

In the previous chapter, you prepared yourself to work on your self-esteem. You received sufficient information to determine whether self-help is for you and whether this is the right time to begin such a programme. You also decided if you wanted to involve a buddy or not.

This chapter will explore the concept of self-esteem more thoroughly. How does CBT look upon it? How can low self-esteem arise and what are its consequences? And, most importantly, what can you do about it?

What is meant by 'self-esteem'?

Self-esteem means the value or worth you place on yourself as a person. It is the way you feel about yourself. It can be high, low or something in between. If you feel you are an okay person, you will have a healthy self-esteem and be confident. If you feel you are not okay, you will have low self-esteem and experience lack of confidence. Social psychologist Morris Rosenberg, who researched self-esteem extensively in the 1960s, discerns several self-esteem components. One of these components is what you 'know' about yourself: rational knowledge. What you know includes your characteristics, your talents, your qualities, your capacities, and your quirks. Another component of self-esteem is the way you view each of these: without being aware of it, you view each of them through a positive or negative lens. You would think that all these things together form your self-esteem. But Rosenberg says that there is a third component: how much importance you attach to each of these qualities.

All kinds of 'unfairness' can sneak into this complicated equation. You may be aware of some of your own qualities, for example, but not all of them. Or you may attach a negative value to characteristics that are deemed positive by most people, and find some areas very important, while others will hardly matter at all. Different people with almost the same 'ingredients' can therefore have a totally different self-esteem. This is why a person who is apparently successful and has many good qualities may still have the conviction, the core belief, 'I am a failure' or 'I am not okay'. While someone else, who is not at all that remarkable, may be quite happy with him or herself.

So, in practice, what is low self-esteem? Your negative core belief is stored in your memory. It is always there. Yet you rarely consider your characteristics or how you value them. You are unlikely to notice how your characteristics, skills, and talents express themselves in the things you do on a daily basis. And you will likely be unaware that you find some characteristics or talents more important than others. What does tend to reach your conscience is a final conclusion or overall opinion of yourself. The emotions you associate with this overall opinion are mostly easily remembered. But even if it does not register consciously, the influence of your core belief is strong. It affects your self-esteem and confidence. It also affects your perception: it is the looking glass through which you view yourself and the world around you.

What if your self-esteem is low?

People with low self-esteem always come to a negative conclusion about themselves – their core belief is negative. For instance, Denise thinks, 'I'm a failure', and Michael's conclusion regarding almost everything he does, is: 'I am worth nothing'. These are more than casual thoughts – each is based on a strong conviction. Each of these thoughts is not followed by a question mark but an exclamation mark!

Such a negative conviction can be activated at any given moment. If you are criticized, for instance, your negative core belief will show itself immediately, like a jack-in-the-box. Other memories that are stored in your memory will join in and tumble over one another. Everything comes back to you: the criticism you received last week, the things you failed at, the things you did not accomplish perfectly. What also comes back are the qualities and meanings you gave to events in the past. Beliefs such as 'I am clumsy' or 'I cannot persevere', 'I am sloppy' or 'I am dumb' crop up again. This prevents you from putting things into perspective. And that is why you once again draw the same conclusion: 'I am worthless'. As this goes hand in hand with strong negative emotions, such as fear, sadness, anger or shame, you store even more negative information, reaffirming your negative conviction.

Do some people have healthy self-esteem?

Yes, they do. Individuals who have healthy self-esteem view themselves realistically. They think they are okay. They believe themselves to be useful despite their flaws (which they acknowledge). They think about their successes a bit more often than about their failures and their positive memories are easier to recall. They recall with ease a good job they did yesterday, for instance, or a problem they solved last week, or a chance meeting they had with someone nice last summer. Positive characteristics join in: they see themselves as independent, resourceful, and good company. And that goes hand in hand with positive feelings. They are able to deflect criticism and are optimistic about their future. They feel confident.

There are others whose self-esteem is too high, they are overconfident. They see themselves in too favourable a light, are unable to face their downsides, and are totally insensitive to criticism. They tend to put themselves 'above the law'. The aim of this book is to help you gain a healthy self-esteem, it is not about becoming overconfident.

Selective perception and selective memory

In CBT, cognitions are often considered the same as 'thoughts': biased thoughts about daily reality or one-sided interpretations. In fact, the 'C' refers to a more complicated mechanism, namely the 'cognitive processing of information': How is incoming information dealt with and how is it archived? Does everything enter the memory and if so, how? Where is it stored? And can you retrieve it again, at a later date? In CBT, a negative core belief is compared to being prejudicial. If you are prejudiced about something, you no longer see things as they really are, because you look at them from a particular angle. Without being aware of it, certain information enters your memory easily whereas other information enters with difficulty or does not enter at all. The effect of this is that you see what you want to unconsciously believe. It is a natural process that everyone experiences and you can only counter it with a concerted effort.

Your memory can be compared to an archive full of large and small boxes. The boxes that are used often are at eye level and easy to access. Those that are rarely used are tucked away at the back. Unfortunately, mistakes are sometimes made during storage, so that many events and experiences end up in the wrong box. This means that during your life, an unnecessarily negative view of yourself may be formed. Once such a negative core belief has been formed, you will see a big box labelled 'I am a failure' as soon as you open the archive's doors. You won't be able to miss it. It is as if you heard a voice: 'Store it here. This is where it belongs, together with all the other failures.' Information relating to your negative conviction reaffirms the prejudice you have about yourself. Positive information that does not fit, like a compliment, goes unnoticed or is distorted in such a way that it can be fitted in after all. This way, you gather more and more negative information and the box labelled 'I am a failure' becomes fuller and fuller.

It is impossible to miss Emma. Her dark blue work uniform accentuates her slim figure, yet she thinks that people don't notice her.

Two days ago she celebrated her forty-eighth birthday, all by herself. Although she had not invited anyone, she was still disappointed that nobody dropped by. She has lost many friends over the years because they got partners and kids. She didn't

2

want to bother them and she soon got the feeling that she was imposing. She has little contact with her five brothers and sisters and her family is disjointed. Emma has no fond memories of her past. Her mother was unable to take care of the family and was often committed to a psychiatric institute. Her father worked hard to make ends meet. The children were often left to their own devices. Aunts and uncles took care of them only sporadically.

When she was nineteen, Emma quit school and left home. There was always work in tourism. Up to the age of thirty-five, she had had all kinds of jobs abroad, and relationships with many different men. Then her big love, Ed, walked into her life. She moved in with him and started working as a receptionist in a big hotel where she still works today. After a couple of years, however, Emma ended their relationship and started living on her own because Ed was repeatedly cheating on her. Since then, she has been sad and she drinks more than she should. She easily becomes angry. Of late, she has been quite irritable.

The information processing of someone with low self-esteem is distinguished by 'unfairness'. Selective perception causes you mostly to see 'failures'. If you do succeed at something, you hardly acknowledge it, or regard it as being of little consequence. Even if you do admit to a small success, there will be many more things you find fault in. Information that does not fit in is remodelled or distorted in such a way that it does fit after all. This is called 'cognitive distortion'.

Selective memory causes you to mostly remember things that fit your negative view of yourself such as criticism you received after a presentation and the meaning you attached to it: 'I must be stupid'. The box marked 'I am a failure' is filling up quickly! (Exercise 2.1 consists of a questionnaire to measure your self-esteem.) The few positive experiences stored in your memory have been placed in one of those small boxes at the back. If you want to store something there, it'll take a lot of effort.

The consequence of selective perception is that you remain trapped in your negative view of yourself. To implement change, you need to don a different pair of glasses and actively search for positive information and other experiences and store them in that small box in the back of the archive. In doing so you will strengthen an alternative positive core belief. You will learn how to do this in Chapters 3, 4, and 5.

Denise does not know how she developed low self-esteem. Maybe it's because she was the only one in her class to do an apprenticeship. She would have loved to study for A-levels, but her parents didn't feel it was worthwhile. Because of this, she lost many of her friends and did not feel at home in school. She really wanted to study, but that was not done in her class. She got her diploma and trained as a tailor's cutter. She worked in a studio for a couple of years and in a community centre for Turkish youths. 'It really wasn't that special, you know', she says. And now she is a playground supervisor: 'Anyone can do that.' Denise likes to be involved in school. She finds it fascinating to see how children learn to read and write. But she does not have the courage to work with reading groups or to apply to be a library mum. What she does do is check the children for head lice: 'They couldn't find anyone else to do that.' She would like to go back to school and move on in life. Her husband Aziz encourages this, but she has not gotten around to it yet: 'I am a failure', she thinks.

It's not all just in your head

An important indication of self-esteem is how someone behaves. Those who feel negatively about themselves behave differently from those who feel positively about themselves. If you are convinced you are dumb, you will not ask questions in a room full of people. If you are convinced you are clumsy, you will leave chores at home to others. Emma, who is convinced nobody notices her, entered each new relationship with a boyfriend passively and asking little for herself. Now she has convinced herself she doesn't want a relationship any more. Recently, Emma has lambasted male colleagues when she felt they were ignoring her.

It is only logical that your behaviour is a consequence of your feelings. Yet, that is not the whole story, as your feelings are just as much a consequence of your behaviour. From observing your own behaviour you draw conclusions about yourself, your personality and your qualities. If you want to strengthen your confidence, you have to do more than learn to look differently at yourself. It is equally important that you start to behave differently. Chapters 6, 7, and 8 will help you develop and strengthen the behaviour that goes with a healthy self-esteem.

2 The causes of low self-esteem

There is no one cause of low self-esteem, as many factors contribute to the development of a person's confidence. We are not yet sure how these factors interact but the following factors are likely influential:

- *Predisposition*. Scientists believe we do not come into the world as a blank canvas. On the contrary, many things are determined by our genes and everyone has a certain predisposition, sensitivity or vulnerability at birth.
- *The family*. Further development of one's self-esteem begins early on, between the first and second year of your life. Unfavourable experiences in childhood include being ignored, receiving little attention and appreciation, getting a lot of criticism, and having demands placed upon you not befitting your age. A competitive atmosphere in the family, being appreciated in one respect only, or constantly being compared with a sibling can engender a feeling of 'not being good enough'. Affective neglect, abuse, and incest often

lead a child to conclude that they are 'bad'. Being raised in an over protective environment, however, can also have negative consequences.

- *School, the environment, peers, significant others.* For some people, growing up among classmates or peers from different backgrounds can make them feel like an outsider. If they are bullied, they are bombarded with negative messages. The bullying is usually not about one aspect of their life, but about them as a whole person.
- *The national character.* Proverbs, mottos, and sayings reflect the core values of society. There are many English sayings that frown upon speaking positively about yourself, including being 'big-headed' or 'too big for your boots'.
- *Your survival strategy.* Many people develop a strategy early in life to protect themselves from failure and rejection as well as having to confront their low self-esteem. This strategy functions as a set of 'rules for living', including guidelines for your behaviour, such as 'make sure that you …, or else …'. However, this won't make the low self-esteem disappear; on the contrary, it will only reaffirm it.

Your self-esteem, then, is a result of what is predetermined in the genes and what you learn in life. Fortunately, a lot more can be learned using this self-help programme.

Lindsey (32) was bullied a lot in primary school because she was the only one in her class with short hair and did not wear the right clothes. When she had long hair and wore the right clothes, there was something else her classmates would find fault with. To avoid the bullying Lindsey tried to be as inconspicuous as possible – she would have loved to have been invisible. For the few friends she had, she really went the extra mile. She tried to please them in every way she could. She succeeded in this and still sees two of them today. She totally immersed herself in her schoolwork – it had to be perfect, as she wanted to be better than the others. She became a vet and worked in a small-animal practice in Bath for a while, but she did not like the contact she had with the pets' owners. That is why she started working for the government. Her department becomes very busy when there is an outbreak of bird flu or swine fever but even when there is no epidemic, there is plenty of work to do.

Lindsey has been at home for two months now. She is really tired and has headaches all the time. She feels worthless but that is nothing new; she has felt like that almost all her life. That feeling is really strong now. She avoids her two friends as she feels she has nothing to offer them anymore now that she is at home. She only tolerates her cats, her dog Daisy, and her husband around her.

2 The consequences of low self-esteem

Since your self-esteem is with you all the time, it influences every aspect of your life.

Low self-esteem can have the following unpleasant consequences:

- *A sombre mood.* If you view yourself from a particular angle, your mood can be negatively affected by it. You become sombre and dispirited, sad or anxious.
- *Less courage.* If you see yourself as worthless, you will be pessimistic about the influence you can exert over your life. You expect to fail sooner or later. That is why you have less courage to take on new or difficult challenges.
- *Little initiative.* If you are sombre and pessimistic about your own abilities, it takes more effort than usual to become active. You do less and avoid more. Additionally, you constantly criticize yourself, which is unhelpful because it only tells you what not to do, not

what you can do, which can lead to what is called 'learned helplessness' – you throw in the towel.

- *Underachievement.* As a consequence of having little initiative, you are less productive and therefore achieve less. This problem is not limited to major things in your life. It affects all kinds of small things that make life more comfortable. A long-term effect of avoidance is that you for go the chance to develop or deploy your skills and so the circle you move in becomes ever smaller.
- *Little self-appreciation.* Because you avoid things a lot and do not undertake that much, there is also less reason to be pleased with, or proud of, yourself and less reason to praise and appreciate yourself.

In this way, you enter a vicious circle – you feel more negative about yourself all the time, which goes to reaffirm your low self-esteem (Figure 2.1).

Figure 2.1 The vicious circle of low self-esteem

For some people, their low self-esteem shows on the outside. They come across as tense, shifty or uninterested. Others do not know what is going on inside and may interpret the outward signals in the wrong way – they may feel that someone like that is hard to approach. Low self-esteem can get in the way of a relationship too: praise from a partner is not recognized, or is distrusted and followed by rejection. Someone with low self-esteem may constantly ask for their partner's approval. In a new relationship, the partner may gladly do so, but often they become tired of it because it is as if their love and appreciation aren't acknowledged.

2

Bryony (32) is the eldest of two children. Her parents had really wanted a son and two years later, their wish came true. Within the family, Bryony was in the shadow of her younger brother Ben. Her parents ordered her to do all kinds of things for him, be considerate to him, and so on. They still do, although Ben has been an adult for a while now and can take care of himself. Ben was praised from an early age, whereas Bryony was criticized a lot and rarely praised. She was often compared to her brother.

'I am a nobody', reads the label on her archive box. The only thing she is occasionally positive about is that she is dedicated and sacrifices herself for others. Her boss gives her a lot of compliments, praises her qualities, and says she is irreplaceable. Bryony thinks that he is exaggerating. Of course she works hard and takes a lot out of his hands, and she is hardly ever sick – but she is not unique in this respect.

What is healthy?

People with healthy self-esteem and a nuanced, positive view of themselves are lucky. Healthy self-esteem protects against negative influences such as depression and other forms of psychological distress. It usually goes hand in hand with success, well-being, and happiness.

Individuals with healthy self-esteem are confident and think of themselves in positive terms, for example 'I am okay' or 'I'm not too bad'. People like this have discovered various positive aspects about themselves, without denying their downsides. They know their strengths, which are connected with all kinds of concrete experiences, events, and actions. This is called 'evidence' in CBT. They are optimistic and assertive. They remain convinced of their positive view, even when things are not going their way. They are also able to take criticism or rejection; although they might feel slightly hurt, it doesn't affect their confidence or change their behaviour drastically. In the archive, there is a big box with a positive label attached that is difficult to miss.

Not everyone is fortunate enough to have a positive view of themselves. If the title of this book appeals to you, chances are that your self-esteem is low and your view of yourself is not very nuanced. Or maybe it is shaky and changes with the circumstances. It can also be rigid, which means that it does not change when you gain new, positive experiences.

How can you enhance your self-esteem and develop your confidence?

The approach described in this book is based on a CBT approach. The goal is to alter both the way you look at yourself and the way you behave, which in turn will change the way you feel about yourself. This approach assumes that what has been archived (your negative core belief) cannot be deleted, but you can add a new positive core belief that can compete with the old one you would love to delete. You need to fill the small unremarkable positive box with positive information to develop a firm positive core belief. This approach does not involve battling negative convictions as the less time you spend on the negative box and the information it contains, the better. That information has been dragged up often enough and the negative box's existence has been affirmed quite enough in the past.

The following chapters will help you to build up a competing positive view of yourself for which you will need a lot of new information. Imagine it as emptying a shelf in the archive on which you then place a box with a positive label: 'I am okay', for instance, or 'I belong'. You will start filling this box with positive information – the more the better and hopefully it will soon be full. The negative box will be attended to less often and have less chance to catch you unawares with negative memories. In Exercise 2.2 you will be asked to choose your own label for the new positive box.

> When Lindsey thinks about her low self-esteem, she immediately thinks 'I am worthless'. It repeats like a mantra. It is not hard to think of the opposite: 'I am somebody' – she thinks that's a good choice of label. Right now, it's difficult for her to believe, but if she can convince herself, 'I am somebody', in a year's time a miracle might happen.
>
> Bryony has more trouble finding a positive label. Like Lindsey, she at first replaces 'I am a nobody' with 'I am somebody'. Somehow, however, it doesn't quite fit and so she eventually chooses, 'It is okay for me to be who I am'.
>
> Michael chooses 'I am okay'. It is short and powerful and it should compete with the old 'Once people really get to know me, I will fall short'.

What do you need to do to enhance your self-esteem and build your confidence? Shouting 'I am okay' a lot won't really help. You have to view yourself from a new angle and learn to notice positive facts (big and small), and reflect on those. You have to do this as often as you can. The step from concrete behaviour, thoughts, and feelings to the conclusion 'I am okay' is, however, a difficult one.

Figure 2.2 Building your self-esteem

'I have done the housework, collected the children from school,
enjoyed the sun and called my elderly aunt, so I am okay', is
unlikely to sound credible to you. That is why you need to learn to
recognize your positive qualities in these everyday experiences.
'I am precise, caring and attentive, and I can enjoy the little
things, so I am okay', sounds quite a bit more convincing.
Strengthening your positive core belief and paying less attention
to the negative one will soon result in healthier self-esteem and
more confidence.

Furthermore, it is important that you start behaving differently as
well. In many cases, this new behaviour will automatically manifest
itself when you learn to view yourself from a different angle, but you
can also help the change process along. Through new behaviour you
gain new experiences and thus positive thoughts and feelings about
yourself. Finally, you have to ensure that the old negative view of
yourself can't raise its ugly head. Initially, it will remain a formidable
competitor, but this book gives you the tools to put your negative
self-image in a dark corner in the archive. To make change visible,
you will be asked to reflect on how convinced you are of your new
positive core belief. In Exercise 2.3, you will be asked to do this for
the first time.

Exercises

Exercise 2.1: Do I have low self-esteem?

To measure how severe your low self-esteem is, complete the Rosenberg Self-Esteem Scale, which was created specifically for this purpose.

* *Time to allow: 10 minutes*
* *How to go about it*

   ✓ Read the list.
   ✓ For each statement, indicate to what degree you agree with it by circling a number in one of columns 2–5.
   ✓ Calculate your total score by summing the numbers you have circled.

2

	Strongly agree	Agree	Dis- agree	Strongly disagree
On the whole, I am satisfied with myself	3	2	1	0
At times I think I am no good at all	0	1	2	3
I feel that I have a number of good qualities	3	2	1	0
I am able to do things as well as most other people	3	2	1	0
I feel I do not have much to be proud of	0	1	2	3
I certainly feel useless at times	0	1	2	3
I feel that I am a person of worth, at least on an equal plane with others	3	2	1	0

I wish I could have more respect for myself	0	1	2	3
All in all, I am inclined to feel that I am a failure	0	1	2	3
I take a positive attitude towards myself	3	2	1	0

Total score: ...

The higher your total score, the more confident you are. A score below 18 indicates low self-esteem, while a score below 15 indicates very low self-esteem.

Exercise 2.2: Formulating a new positive core-belief
Low self-esteem arises when you draw a negative conclusion about yourself. This can be a short statement starting with 'I am ...', such as 'I am a failure'. The positive self-image you need to build will serve as its competitor. It demands that you formulate a short and powerful riposte.

* *Time to allow: 20 minutes*
* *How to go about it*

  ✓ Write down the negative statement that comes to mind when you think about yourself.
  ✓ Now think of a positive statement. It has to fit you and be short and powerful. It is best to take the opposite of the old negative statement: 'I am okay' as opposed to 'I am an idiot'. A double negation ('I am not dumb') won't work well and you will never believe in statements that are too positive ('I am fantastic!').
  ✓ Strike through the old negative statement.

My negative self-image:
....

My new positive core belief:
....

Exercise 2.3: Rating the credibility of your new core belief

At the end of each chapter, you will reflect on the steps you have already taken and how this has affected your self-esteem.

- *Time to allow: 2 minutes*
- *How to go about it*

  ✓ Write the statement representing your new core belief on the dotted line.
  ✓ Indicate with a cross how convinced you are of your new core belief.

My new positive core belief (see **Exercise 2.2, page 39**):
....

Date:
Credibility:

2

:——:——:——:——:——:——:——:——:——:——:
0   10   20   30   40   50   60   70   80   90   100

0 = not at all credible   100 = highly credible

3
The positive
data log

In the previous chapter, you learned about the origin and consequences of low self-esteem and how you can do something about it. The following chapters show you how you can build up a positive view of yourself step-by-step.

In this chapter, you will learn to discover positive things about yourself. By looking at things from a different angle, you will find out all kinds of facts about yourself – both big and small – that you will be asked to write down in a positive data log. In combination with the steps described in the following chapters, you will be able to put the old negative view of yourself behind you.

Looking at things from a different angle

Up to now, you have tended to focus mainly on negative issues, something of which you are a bit of an expert. People with low self-esteem notice negative issues ahead of positive ones. The information that fits the negative view of yourself seems to be absorbed more easily. What does not fit in – things that are positive – are not so easily absorbed, or are brushed aside with ease. People with low self-esteem also develop a habit of seeking out negative issues that are not apparent at first glance – like archaeologists, they eagerly carry on digging until they find them. They make much of each negative fact, however small it is. They go over it with a fine-tooth comb and they ponder it, going over it in their minds time after time.

The idea is to apply this method to positive issues from now on. This means looking at yourself in a different way and searching for as many positive facts as you can. Detect, dig, and burrow for them and exaggerate them. Even if they seem trivial at the time, make a habit of emphasizing and repeating them. Also, make a habit of appreciating and praising yourself. In this way, you will be able to gather information to compete with your negative core belief. In other words, you begin to fill a new box in your archive – and the fuller it

Figure 3.1 Changes in a positive direction

gets, the better. Initially, you will find this process difficult and it will feel a little artificial, but eventually your efforts will be rewarded: you will feel better, become more active, and undertake to do more things. If you do this, you will have more to look back on, allowing you to view yourself in a more positive light.

After a while, it will become easier to notice and feel the positive things about yourself. But you must persist until it becomes second nature to you, and keeping a positive data log will help you to do so.

Writing down positive facts has yet another beneficial effect: writing down something positive about your behaviour and feeling good about it can feel like a reward (this is known as 'reinforcement'). From 'learning theory', one of CBT's pillars, we know that a reward strengthens the behaviour that came before it and the chance of your repeating that behaviour is increased. Examples include getting up on time and taking good care of yourself, not avoiding a birthday party despite feeling anxious, taking the time to play with your son or daughter, and applying for a job. When you praise yourself, the likelihood that you will do so again increases. Vocalizing appreciation gives you direction: you know what to do to receive pleasure in similar circumstances in the future. Criticism is the opposite of this, as it indicates only what you shouldn't do. When you start practising new behaviour in Chapter 6, and you are able to praise yourself for it, you will learn quickly.

Writing in your positive data log

What should you write in your positive data log? The answer is, a lot! You could record what was good about your day, what felt good, and what you were successful at. If you were proud of or satisfied about something, write it down. Also record what made you happy, even if it was for only a moment or so. In addition, you should also record any praise or thanks you get from others. The more complete your notes, the better. Your notes can be short – you do not have to make fancy stories out of them. It is important that when you read your notes back to yourself, you are able to recall clearly the pleasant feelings you experienced previously.

3

Lindsey knows a little shop that sells beautiful stationery and she indulges herself by buying a notepad for her positive data log. The first day, she searches for anything positive to record with her husband Kevin. 'Got up on time and took the bus to town [*it had been a long time since she had done that*]. I bought a beautiful notepad and drank a cup of coffee. I took Daisy the dog out three times: twice for a short walk, once for a long one.' She has got five points already! She does find it hard, however, to describe her feelings. She mostly writes down 'satisfied'. 'I read the paper [*for the first time in a long time, due to problems concentrating*], I lay down for a bit [*on the advice of her doctor*], but not all afternoon, I cooked a meal. That is eight.' 'And you were good humoured', says Kevin. Nine points!

One week on, Lindsey writes in the positive data log on a daily basis. It is almost as if she undertakes more in order to be able to write things down. Is that actually the intention? 'No problem', says Kevin, 'becoming more active is good for you. If the notepad helps you with this, that's a bonus. Just take care you do not take on too much at once.'

In your positive data log, you should write about things you are satisfied with or events that gave you a positive feeling. 'But that is the problem', you might argue. 'When do I ever experience a positive feeling? Hardly ever, really. Negative feelings I have in abundance, but I am not allowed to write them down.' That is, indeed, the problem. At first, every positive feeling will be overwhelmed by all kinds of negative thoughts and memories. So you have to pay close attention. Even if you feel it for just a moment, a split second say, if you feel positive, satisfied or proud (before that feeling is killed off by something negative you think of right afterwards), you have something that you can write down. Then, think of what preceded that positive feeling. What event made you happy? What were you proud of? What satisfied you? It can be something you have done (e.g. 'called my mum today because she had to visit the doctor and was nervous about doing so'); something you said ('I complimented my colleague on his new jacket'); something you didn't say ('I was wise to keep my mouth shut when my neighbour once again started to complain about "those rude youngsters"'); something you accomplished ('I finally went for a run again'), or an experience that wasn't necessarily an accomplishment ('I enjoyed the first blooms of spring'). Remember, statements such as 'I am fantastic!' and 'It went alright today' are too vague. Make them more concrete by thinking of why you felt fantastic for a while, or why things went alright.

It is best if you carry your positive data log around with you so that you can make a note as soon as you experience something positive. If you find this inconvenient, you can scribble on any scrap of paper and make your notes properly that night. Because your memory is selective, chances are that you won't remember anything positive that occurred that morning unless you write it down. However, you will notice that as time goes by, it becomes easier to recall positive things.

3

> Michael is thinking of keeping his positive data log on the computer at work. He sits behind a screen for a large part of his working day and can therefore easily make notes. In the evening he'll clean up his 'catch of the day' as he has come to call it and add to it as well. His girlfriend Caroline will be able to read along too, which is a great plan! The following day, however, he notes a few obstacles to his plan, as he is often busy, away from his desk or suspects a colleague of looking over his shoulder. In particular, he doesn't want Kim or Aaron to pry. He sleeps on it and decides to make notes at his desk after all, but finds it hard to record anything positive. Michael assumes that he will learn to do so.

It's good to consult your positive data log on a regular basis. You can set aside time to do so, at the end of the day, for instance. Re-read the notes of the past few days and if you recall something, add it to your log. On less happy days when you don't identify many positives, reading your positive data log can help you recall the pleasant feelings you had when making the notes.

> Bryony is looking in her closet for some old notebooks that are lying around somewhere. She is keen to get to work on her positive data log. The first week she does not succeed in writing

anything down. She has an aversion to doing so, as she finds writing down positive things about herself uncomfortable. The memory of her brother being praised to the hilt all the time keeps entering her mind: he never faced criticism. She notices that if something positive does occur to her, she gets quite tense and the second week is no different.

Getting started

All things are difficult before they become easy. Do not be surprised if you cannot think of positive things to record in the first week, as it is vastly different from what you are used to. Most often, any positive feelings are already over before you really notice them, and now you have to actually consider your happy, proud or satisfied feelings and record them too! It'll probably take months before something like this becomes second nature to you. Do not despair, press on. You will notice after a couple of weeks that it starts to get easier.

Michael wants Karim to be his buddy. They have been friends for a long time. They know each other from high school, run together twice a week, and afterwards grab a bite to eat at Michael's. They are training for a half-marathon. Karim is quite different from Michael, and is much more laid back.

Michael has already begun keeping his positive data log and his girlfriend Caroline reads it. He writes little the first few days, but when he is still not producing after a week, he asks Caroline to help him. She can't understand why he doesn't know what to say and thinks that there are all kinds of things from work that could be recorded in his positive data log. She proposes going over that day. What did he do? Did nothing special happen all day? There was indeed something special: a new computer system. Everyone had attended a course beforehand, but

3

Michael had attended a second one because he is a 'super user'. And today was the big day. He guessed he would need to be there to help his colleagues all day, and that was the case, since many things were unclear to them. He was about to highlight all that went wrong, when Caroline interrupted him: 'I think we have some positive things here already.' 'Okay', he said, 'I ensured that I had no other engagements all day.' 'Good, write that down', says Caroline: 'Anything else?' 'I helped when there were problems, I did not lose my patience, I had cake delivered in the afternoon, and I thanked everyone for their efforts at the end of the day', Michael sums up, aided by Caroline.

And yes, there is something else for his positive data log: he phoned his sick colleague, Astrid, at the end of the morning. She got the results from a blood test today and was worried. He writes: 'I phoned her, and she really appreciated it. I let her tell her story. I let her know that I am thinking of her. I asked her if she would like me to visit without pressuring her.' 'Great!', says Caroline.

When writing things down you are proud of, happy with or grateful for, all kinds of additional thoughts can get in the way. Maybe you were made to feel at an early age that it is wrong to think positively about yourself. So if thinking something positive is already bad, then writing it down or saying it out loud really is taboo. Yet it is better to ignore such 'rules'. Think again why you are doing this and what you have to gain from thinking positively about yourself.

Another problem is that although you may identify 'positive' things about yourself, you may not 'feel' positively about them. For example, you know 'objectively' that running a half-marathon is a great achievement, but you feel no pride. And isn't it supposed to be about you yourself feeling positive about what you record in your positive data log? Surely writing things down because you know that someone else will be impressed cannot be the intention? Don't worry, as eventually your feelings like your mind will come to realize that something is good. But it'll take time. Feelings are like a tortoise lagging behind the hare, but they do get there in the end!

Agnieszka has bought a beautiful little booklet with a cloth cover. 'Exactly my colours', she thinks to herself, 'and small enough to take with me in my purse'. She thinks writing will be fun, but in practice she is disappointed. It just doesn't work during the day, so she has to do it at night. The first couple of days, she sits down to do it after dinner and tries to recall what happened that day but comes to the conclusion that it was all quite normal.

Luckily, she talks to Paul about the problems she was experiencing in her training. She has known Paul since nursery school and, just like Agnieszka, he is not a particularly easy-going person. She tells him she is trying to boost her self-esteem with a self-help programme. She also tells him she does not know what to write in her positive data log, so Paul helps her start by picking a few concrete things from her story he finds positive. 'You chatted with your colleague', he says. 'That seems really good to me. And you comforted that old lady and stayed with her for a while. Go ahead and write that down.' He tells her she judges herself too harshly, something he recognizes immediately, as it's the sort of thing he does himself! Together, they decide to be less harsh on themselves in the future.

Eight ways to enter more facts in your positive data log

The box in the archive reserved for your positive collection needs to be filled with many positive facts, so that eventually it becomes full and you require a bigger box! Once you become accustomed to keeping a positive data log and you no longer feel that you have to make a tremendous effort, you can challenge yourself to discover more and more. Below are some tips.

- *Lower your standards*. Pay attention to all facts and events, even the smallest ones. Appreciate yourself for the effort you put in instead of just looking at the results.
- *Dissect something big into several smaller facts*. Often you can dissect positive data log events into smaller facts. Reflect on all the things you had to do to accomplish something important. Run through it again and write down each component.
- *Take the circumstances into account*. Your mood and condition will change from day to day, so it is wise to adapt your demands to that fact. Formulate it as follows: 'Despite being sombre, I still managed to ...'. That makes it easier to discover something positive.
- *Repetition is important*. Remember, you are allowed to record an event that you have written about before. Try not to see things you used to find hard or things you did not dare to do as matters of course. They are still special and the trick is to keep noticing them.
- *Make it personal*. Many people with low self-esteem find it hard to detect their contribution to any pleasant event. Ask yourself what your contribution was. Surely you had something to do with the fact that it was a great atmosphere or that others were kind to you.
- *Block out negative mind talk*. You have probably noticed that when you have written down something positive, you feel a strong tendency to add something negative. You are very good at trivializing or giving little value to positive events. This counteracts the positive, so you should aim not to do so. Chapter 5 deals at length with negative mind talk.
- *Look at it another way for once*. You should realize that there is more to life than achievements and dedication to others. Pay attention to other areas of life, such as enjoyment, assertiveness,

hobbies, your relationship with your partner, sports you enjoy, your appearance, laughter, relaxation, and so on.

- *Pay attention to what you find hard to do.* Pay special attention to daily inhibitions in your positive data log. If you find it hard to relax, for instance, you can focus on times when you did manage to relax, even if it was for a short time.

It will not be possible to apply all these tips at the same time. One will probably appeal to you more than the others, so start with it, or the one that you expect to result in the largest increase in positive facts. After a while you can apply another tip. Attempt as many as possible in an effort to discover which approach provides the best results.

In the third week, Bryony writes a few lines in her positive data log. She does so reluctantly, as she has many reservations about the things she writes down, even about the compliments her boss pays her. She has worked as a secretary for an advertising agency for five years now and is her boss's right hand. Over time, she has been given more tasks and responsibilities. She sort of runs her own part of the workplace now and she does so very well. 'But what does that amount to, really?', she often thinks. That question arises again when her boss tells her once more how much he appreciates her. She cannot help herself – it drives her crazy. She understands she has to stop reducing herself to zero.

Just at the right moment, her cousin Bibi, who she gets on well with, asks her what is wrong. Bryony explains what the problem is and together they go through the list of tips and pick one: dissect something big into several smaller facts.

With a great deal of effort, Bryony manages to distill a task that she completed successfully to a half page full of facts. The PR material she drew up for a client came in today. And it was totally perfect. She hesitatingly admits that she felt proud.

She thinks of what steps she had to take: finding out what the client wanted exactly, getting to the bottom of the company´s philosophy, conducting interviews, writing texts, having photos taken, managing the designer and printer, consulting twenty times, and correcting proofs. So, if you follow this process, the positive data log almost writes itself.

Persisting and continuing

Some people are enthusiastic about starting a self-help programme only for them to quit after a few weeks. In the beginning, it is new and exciting and they have a clear idea of why they are doing it. Soon, however, they come to realize that keeping a positive data log takes effort and that their self-esteem won't improve over night! Their negative conviction simmers away close to the surface and disappointment is never far away.

The best way to persist is to make writing in your positive data log a regular activity. You can prevent forgetting positive things by writing down events as they happen or as soon after as possible. And you can add to the day's notes at a set time in the evening, for example. At the outset, a buddy can act as your motivator. Once you realize that by writing down positive things your mood changes, you will do it more often and more easily. Do take care that it doesn't become a boring task. Making a few notes on autopilot at the end of the day without letting that pleasant feeling in will be of little use. If that is the way things are going, you might consider taking a week out from completing the positive data log. Having a break will enable you to start afresh. You can also add variety by focusing on things at work one week, household things the next, and contacts with friends the week after that. Focus on achievements one week and focus on relaxation and enjoyment the next. Once you notice you have begun to regularly praise yourself without any effort, you can proceed without the aid of the positive data log. On average, it takes six months to do this but for some it will take less time and for others it may take a bit longer.

'Isn't that book too small for everything you write down now?', Kevin teases Lindsey when she reads from her data log. Last week, they discussed how Lindsey could write more in her book because when she started working a couple of half days a week again, she became less productive. The conclusion was: you have to lower your standards, the phrase 'matter of course' must be deleted from your dictionary.

It is not a matter of course that she joins her colleagues for lunch. She has not done so for years. It is brave of her to do so and she now feels part of the group, which does not come easy to her. A good tip for her is to dissect something big into several smaller facts. When writing you experience them again, which she thinks gives you a good feeling. Another tip she wants to adopt is to vary what she writes about. She doesn't want to focus solely on work and contacts with friends, but also the care she gives her pets and her elderly neighbours, the cakes she bakes (her hobby) and, most importantly, the attention she pays to Kevin. If she follows up on all her intentions, the notebook will soon be full.

Exercises

Exercise 3.1: Writing in your positive data log

Record events and experiences in your log that you have positive feelings about – everything that makes you proud, happy or satisfied, even if only for a little while. By doing this, you learn to view yourself in a positive way.

- *Time to allow: 30 minutes*
- *How to go about it*

    ✓ Record something in your positive data log every day.
    ✓ Do this as soon as possible after the event.
    ✓ Re-read your notes from previous days on a regular basis.
    ✓ Read your positive data log when you feel sombre or sad.

Example: Lindsey's notes on day 1 of her log

Date + time	Positive data log event	Feeling
Tuesday 20 October		
8 a.m.	got up on time	satisfied
11 a.m.	took the bus to the city (it's been a long time)	satisfied
	bought a beautiful notepad	happy
	drank a cup of coffee	?
2 p.m.	lay down on the bed (doctor's orders)	satisfied
5 p.m.	read the newspaper (has been a long time, owing to poor concentration)	happy because I succeeded
6 p.m.	cooked a meal	happy
	good mood (says Kevin)	
	walked Daisy 3x	

Exercise 3.2: Writing more in your positive data log

Looking at yourself in a positive way is a skill that can be honed. There are many ways to increase the number of notes you make in your positive data log.

- *Time to allow: 15 minutes*
- *How to go about it*

  ✓ Check which tips appeal to you.
  ✓ Pick one or two tips you want to focus on for now.
  ✓ Choose another one or two after a couple of weeks.
  ✓ View the increase in writing output as a challenge, not a demand.

A list of tips to increase the number of notes you make

- Lower your standards.
- Dissect something big into several smaller facts.
- Take circumstances into account.
- The repetition of facts is perfectly okay.
- Discover what your own part was in positive events.
- Stop negative mind talk.
- Find new areas to consider.
- Pay particular attention to things you find hard to do.

In the following weeks, I want to try the following tips:

....

....

Exercise 3.3: Rating the credibility of your new core belief

Reflect on the steps you have already taken and how this has affected your self-esteem.

- *Time to allow: 2 minutes*
- *How to go about it*

✓ Copy the positive statement you wrote in **Exercise 2.2 (page 39).**
✓ Indicate with a cross how convinced you are of your new core belief.

My new positive core belief:

....

Date:
Credibility:

:——:——:——:——:——:——:——:——:——:——:
0   10   20   30   40   50   60   70   80   90   100

0 = not at all credible   100 = highly credible

3

4
Positive qualities

In the previous chapter, you looked at things from a different angle. You learned to pay more attention to positive issues than to negative ones. You started to praise yourself in the positive data log on daily events that you would not have considered positive before.

In this chapter, you take the next step by thinking about what the positive data log events say about who you are as a person. You no doubt have as many good, fun, and pleasant qualities as anybody else; you just have to learn to see and acknowledge them.

What does your behaviour say about you?

If you have low self-esteem, you likely interpret all kinds of situations in an unfavourable way, even those that have nothing to do with you. If your colleague is cranky (because unbeknown to you he had an argument with his wife this morning), you may well blame yourself for his demeanour: 'I'm really slow to grasp things. I ask his advice too often. I really am not fit for this job.' You no doubt can think of some examples of your own.

When building up a healthy self-esteem, you have to learn to think of situations in a positive way. You have already learned to pay attention to positive behaviour, events, and experiences, so the next step is to become aware of the positive qualities that are needed for these experiences. If you go for a run after three bad nights' sleep, you may consider yourself 'disciplined' or a 'winner'. And if your colleague fails to listen to you and you manage to put that aside, you might think yourself 'thick-skinned' or 'laconic'. Although you don't always react like this, you do possess the quality to do so. The idea is that you look for positive qualities in everyday events – the more, the better. All these qualities together form a positive and beautifully nuanced view of yourself. Exercise 4.1 will help you make a start.

Adding positive qualities to your positive data log

The events and experiences you record in your positive data log form the starting point. You should be able to think of positive attributes for some achievements, although thinking of more than one quality might not be so easy. It becomes more difficult for events and experiences that are not an achievement, such as having enjoyed a day at the beach, but you should be able to add some personal meaning to such an experience too.

How do you go about doing this? At a set time at the end of the day, for example, think of positive qualities for the events you have recorded in your positive data log. You do not have to think of qualities for every entry, simply pick a few that appeal to you. For 'built a rabbit hutch for my daughter', you could think of qualities such as 'handyman', 'technical', 'caring', 'good parent', 'animal lover', and so on. You do not have to formulate it neatly, as it is not necessary to describe the quality in a single word – a sentence is just as good. A simple fact, such as building a rabbit hutch, is the starting point for thinking of positive traits or talents. And these talents have associations of their own with positive events and experiences from the past.

Begin with events that immediately make you think of some of your positive qualities. Later, when you are more experienced at this exercise, you can choose an event that is not directly related to your qualities: 'seen a good movie on TV', for instance. Ask yourself what this says about you. You might conclude that you are a movie lover, maybe even a movie buff, or that you are someone who can enjoy simple things, someone who takes care of him or herself.

If you do this on a regular basis, it will become much easier to highlight your different qualities, and taking the step to 'I am okay' or 'I belong' won't seem quite so preposterous.

4

Agnieszka's positive data log fills up despite the fact that she found it difficult to identify anything positive at first. Paul put her on the right track and now she writes every day about what satisfies her and makes her happy. She even wrote down once that she was proud of herself! She likes to think of qualities for the events she recorded and put them in a word circle. Having got a good grade for a report today, 'precise' is the first quality that came to mind. She worked on the report for some time and looked up all the jargon in her study books and on the internet. 'Punctual' she thinks. She's almost the only one of her class who handed in her report on time. But isn't punctual the same as precise? 'Hardworking' she thinks, and 'interested'. And oh yeah, 'motivated'. She really puts effort into everything she does!

When she goes through the positive data log with Paul, he notices the qualities all have to do with achievements, hard work, and having good evaluations. In the meantime, she doesn't believe she is valuable to others: 'I do not belong' is her old phrase. Paul thinks she should write down more things in her positive data log that have to do with fitting in. Has she experienced anything worth mentioning in that respect? 'This is a little like a cross-examination', Agnieszka says, but Paul ignores that remark and waits to see if she can come up with something. Agnieszka recalls that the day before yesterday, after her shift had ended, she had a chat with one of the nurses who had been sick for a long time. She doesn't know exactly what feeling this gave her, but it was pleasant. Together they make a word circle (Figure 4.1).

Agnieszka thinks it all a bit exaggerated. It looks great on paper, but she is not yet convinced.

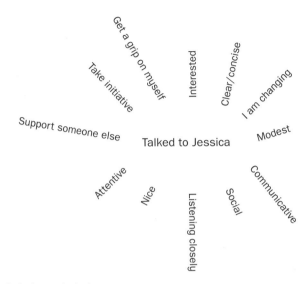

Figure 4.1 A word circle

The positive qualities list

After a couple of weeks, you will have recorded many positive qualities in your positive data log. The next step is to highlight them and form a list of the positive qualities you have. This document, also called your 'psychological passport', describes who you are, what distinguishes you, what your strengths are, and what makes you special. The profile that emerges will be a little nuanced. But the idea is not to stop there. No doubt, the list can be extended, so that your positive view of yourself becomes even more versatile.

You can draw up such a list at the back of your positive data log. Reserve a couple of pages for it because it might get quite long! Some people like to use a separate piece of paper, but do whatever suits you. Agnieszka, for instance, writes every quality on a card and watches the stack grow each week.

The idea is that you keep adding to your positive qualities list. When giving meaning to facts from your positive data log, you will come across new qualities all the time. Exercise 4.2 will show you how to do that. The praise and appreciation of others can help you too.

Getting started

Making a positive list can be an odd task: 'It's going a bit far blowing one's own trumpet', you might think. Writing down your positive qualities seems odd enough, but saying them out loud seems a step too far. You may feel all kinds of objections, even the need to highlight some negative qualities to create some sort of equilibrium.

4

But by thinking up more positive qualities, you get a more nuanced view of yourself in which your downsides become less influential. You will discover that some qualities will be more prominent in one situation and others in another situation, and that some qualities may even be 'dormant', even though you do possess them. The notion of quality may be thought of broadly, in that anything that makes you different, anything that is typically you, or just is part of who you are can be seen as a quality.

After hesitating for some time, Emma has decided to speak with her sister. She is not used to sharing problems with others but plodding on alone isn't helping. Her sister is the only one of her family who she has regular contact with and during a short holiday at Geri's in Spain, she decides to take the plunge. In particular, Emma needs help thinking up her qualities and she and Geri start skyping each other every week.

Today, Emma goes through last week's positive data log and tries to think of qualities herself for the things she has written down before talking to Geri. 'Had a good time working' is the first entry; 'satisfied' is written below it in brackets. 'I am a hard worker' and 'I am service-oriented', she writes below that. 'Did not snap at Jack', she reads. She is very proud of that, but she can't think of any quality to go with it. 'Laughed with' – what was that all about again? Oh yes, she remembers, a funny incident with a supplier. 'Sense of humour': can you say something like that about yourself? That is something to consult Geri on. 'At least I can be relaxed every now and then', Emma thinks, 'but how do I write that down? There are times when I'm not relaxed.' She makes a decision: 'Can be relaxed'. The following is not so hard. 'Helped many guests' results in: 'Friendly, service-oriented, fast, I am good at languages, I know how to comfort people.' 'Cooked for myself', what should I say about that? 'Take care of my health', is that okay? But surely everyone does that? She will consult Geri on this and is curious if she has anything to add.

Geri certainly has something to add. For the 'Jack incident', Geri suggests: 'Tactful, self-controlled, strong, not afraid to set boundaries, stands up for herself.' Emma would never have thought of those herself; she is often tactless and of late she has lost her self-control on occasion. And maybe she *can* set boundaries and stand up for herself, but she rarely does so.

Two months later, Emma has a list of fifty qualities. Friendly, service-oriented, hardworking, tactful, good at languages, fast, loyal to her job, flexible, the ability to adapt, well dressed, groomed, can remember faces, can solve problems, stress-resistant, adventurous, loves to travel, good sense of humour, relaxed, can relax, keeps good health, rarely ill, strong, active, has quit smoking, can comfort people, can indicate boundaries, can stand up for herself, has gained a good position, has a nice house, has a beautiful balcony full of flowers, is a good neighbour, good sister to Geri, interested, good listener, can keep a secret really well, good figure, beautiful hands, dimples in her cheeks when she laughs, environmentally friendly, loves nature, hiker, romantic, can stand being tickled, well organized, finances in good order, handy, does many chores, perseverant, can easily get out of bed, not afraid to show her weaknesses. Every time Emma reads the list, sarcastic remarks present themselves, but this happens less and less often.

Eight ways to add more qualities to your positive list

A healthy, positive view of yourself is nuanced and means you are able to look at yourself from different perspectives. You can, for instance, appreciate yourself for your social attitude because you are always there for your colleagues, always remember your friends' birthdays, and pay attention to people when they converse with you. At the same time, you praise yourself because you guard your boundaries well. You say 'no' to taking more work on if you have too much on your plate already. Having been secretary of your sports club for three years, you decide to quit, even though you are put under pressure not to do so.

When Denise asked her to be her buddy, Gizem said 'yes' immediately. Gizem thinks her neighbour is special. She is quiet and sensible, very warm, and she has fun ideas for the school. 'I am valuable', Gizem suggests, but Denise thinks that too strong. After a little negotiation, they agree on 'I am good enough'.

Now Denise has to identify enough positive qualities to start believing that she is indeed 'good enough'. She takes a large piece of paper and leafs through her positive data log. She has added her positive qualities to the events she has recorded for a couple of weeks now. She copies them down: 'Kind, friendly, attentive ("you have eyes in the back of your head", they say at school), willing to help, thinking up fun games, kind mother, great cook, good housewife.'

Together with Gizem she goes over the tips that can help her extend her list. Gizem says she should think about her previous work. After finishing an apprenticeship as a tailor's cutter (she would have loved to work for her A-levels but her parents thought it unnecessary), she worked in a workshop for a couple of years, which is why she can sew well and draw patterns. When she married Aziz, she wore a wedding dress that she had made herself and designed the bridesmaids' dresses as well. 'So you can design as well', Gizem concludes, 'and you also have fashion-sense. You could easily design costumes for the school party.' After getting married, Denise started to work in a community centre for Turkish youths until her first son was born. They thought she was a good counsellor. She had lots of patience and managed most often to adopt the right tone. She was interested in and keen to hear their stories.

'Your looks', Gizem asks, 'what do you like about those?' 'Great hair', Denise scribbles down right away; she has been told that a lot, and she is happy with her straight hair. 'Aside from that, nothing, I am just average.' Gizem adds 'beautiful eyes, beautiful mouth, great figure ...'. 'Enough, enough!', Denise shouts, 'we have to get the kids, we're running late!'

The more qualities, characteristics, traits, skills, and talents you can think of, the more nuanced your positive view of yourself will become. Below are tips on how to add more qualities to your positive list.

• *Broaden your thinking.* Many things qualify as 'qualities'. You can discover new qualities by finishing the following sentences with words or phrases that are worthy and apply to you: 'I love ...', 'I have ...', 'I am ...', 'I can ...', 'I put great value in ...', 'I believe in ...', 'I feel good when ...', and so on.

- *Research different areas of life.* Everyone has various roles and functions in life, and different traits, skills, and qualities play a role in these different areas. Which aspects of your personality are relevant to each area? What do you love, what do you find enjoyable? What do you think is beautiful about yourself, or funny? And why wouldn't you be proud of the fact that you are smart?
- *Browse dictionaries.* Do not hesitate to add words that are synonyms to your list. They may describe roughly the same quality, but each emphasizes something slightly different about you.
- *Crib from others.* Look at how others present themselves, such as in personal profiles on the internet. Ask yourself whether you possess some positive quality of theirs. Quickly add it to your list if you think you do!
- *Lower your standards.* You do not have to be nice to others all the time to consider yourself a nice person. You do not have to act assertively at all times to consider yourself assertive. Lower your standards a little and check whether you have a quality you hadn't previously considered.
- *Exactly the opposite.* You can extend your positive list by exploring the opposite of all the qualities you have written down so far. So, for 'kind' you might come up with 'strict', 'fierce' or 'consistent'. If you consider you possess one of those qualities, add it to your list. Sometimes it takes a little effort to formulate an opposite quality in a positive way.
- *Reverse roles.* People with low self-esteem are often good at pointing out positive qualities in others. Try to formulate a strong impression of what it is you appreciate in others, and then ask yourself whether you have those qualities too.
- *Ask others for help.* Ask your partner, father, mother, sister, brother, friend, colleague or buddy to make a list for you. You will be amazed at how much they enjoy helping you.

Exercise 4.3 will ask you to choose the tips that appeal to you.

Allow your positive qualities to come to you automatically

At first when you try to think of positive qualities, you may find it very difficult. In time, you will get used to reflecting on your strong and kind side but you can go a step further and immerse yourself. This is nothing to be frightened of – it simply means you do not have to think consciously about what positive qualities you have all the time. They will come to you automatically.

Your belief in your positive qualities will become stronger by revisiting them often. In particular, repetition when under pressure of time contributes to the process of learning by heart or 'making things automatic'. It's just like when at primary school you had to learn things by rote.

All it takes is a minute a day, a piece of paper, and a stopwatch. In that minute, you write down as many of your positive qualities as you can think of. Your goal is to write down ever more qualities within a minute. If you repeat the exercise daily, after a while you will be able to write them down quickly, without any doubts or reservations. This task is addressed in Exercise 4.4.

Steve likes writing. He always has a notepad with him and if he sees something interesting in the paper or on TV, he makes a note. He writes about fantasies and ideas. He picks out an attractive notepad with a marbled cover for the positive data log. It's less effort than he thought keeping his positive data log. In class, with thirty kids demanding his attention, he can't do it during the day, so he waits until the evening to write.

Steve finds it challenging expanding on his positive qualities. 'I am handy', he thinks when he sifts through his log at night and reads that he fixed Chris's bike. Next to that entry, he has written 'satisfied'. 'But not so handy that I could make a living of it', is the thought that next comes to mind. 'I am helpful', he thinks, 'but she did have to nag ten times before I did anything'.

4

After a couple of weeks, when he finds it easier to think up several qualities for the events recorded in his positive data log, he starts to compile his positive list. He can easily identify twenty positive qualities in his log but expanding on them is more difficult. He asks his daughters for help: what do they find good about him? 'Kind', says Marie 'you can read beautifully and you tell fun stories, I think you are a fun teacher'. Chris says she has fun with Steve and that Steve can 'help out really well if you have problems' – but, thinks Steve, 'I can't solve my own problems'.

After another couple of weeks, Steve feels the time has come to start on the one-minute exercise. His positive list contains forty qualities now. Colleagues have suggested a few ('well-read', 'go-getter', 'courageous') and even his ex Helen said some positive things ('flexible', 'perseveres', 'he is a good father'). He is still far from really believing in it: 'Time to immerse yourself!', Steve thinks. He thinks of just four qualities the first day, one of which he wastes seconds on doubting whether he really has that quality after all. A week later, the doubt has subsided and he thinks of ten qualities in a minute – more than double. So he's decided to persevere – he may be a go-getter after all!

Persisting and continuing

At some point, you will feel the need to say something negative, for example: 'I am convinced that I am a hard worker and I am handy and inventive, but I don't work fast enough.' It is best to try and put any such criticism aside for now. Later, you will learn to look at many qualities you deem to be negative from a different angle and you won't be so harsh in your judgement. You may see them in a neutral light or even see them as qualities that also have their good sides. Later, when your confidence has grown, there will be sufficient time to address issues you are less happy with.

Exercises

Exercise 4.1: Adding positive qualities to your positive data log

To start believing in your new-found core belief, you have to learn to connect some conclusion about your positive qualities to concrete behaviour and experiences.

* *Time to allow: 15 minutes a week*
* *How to go about it*

    ✓ Write in your positive data log on a daily basis: record events and your feelings.
    ✓ Think of what the events say about you. If you like, make a word circle with your qualities.
    ✓ Read entries from previous days on a regular basis.

Example: Notes from Emma's positive data log

Date + time	Event	Feeling	Meaning
28 August	had a good time working	satisfied	hard worker service-oriented
	not snapping at Jack	proud	
29 August	had a laugh with Nordin	happy	sense of humour can be relaxed
	helped guests	?	friendly service-oriented good at languages know how to comfort others

Exercise 4.2: Constructing a positive qualities list

Make a list of your qualities as if you were writing a 'psychological passport'. Start this exercise after you have been doing Exercise 4.1 for a couple of weeks.

- *Time to allow: 30 minutes*
- *How to go about it*

  ✓ Think of how you are going to compile your positive list.
  ✓ Copy positive qualities you have written down in your positive data log.
  ✓ Add qualities you highlight when you describe events in your positive data log.
  ✓ Read through the list on a regular basis, especially if you are sombre or sad.

My positive qualities:

....
....
....
....
....
....
....
....
....
....

Exercise 4.3: Possibilities for expansion

You can expand the positive qualities list in several ways.

- *Time to allow: 30 minutes a week*
- *How to go about it*

  ✓ Highlight the tips that appeal to you.
  ✓ Pick one or two of these tips to apply next week.
  ✓ Repeat this after a couple of weeks.
  ✓ View expanding your positive list as a challenge, not a task.

A list of tips to expand the positive qualities list

- ✓ Think more broadly: 'I am good at ...', 'I love ...', 'I enjoy ...', 'I possess ...'.
- ✓ Research different areas of your life.
- ✓ Identify synonyms.
- ✓ Learn from others.
- ✓ Lower your standards.
- ✓ Investigate the opposite.
- ✓ Research what you appreciate in others.
- ✓ Ask others to help you.

In the following weeks, I want to try the following tips:

....

....

Exercise 4.4: Memorizing positive qualities: the one-minute method

Your belief in your positive qualities will grow stronger by repeating them often. In particular, repetition when under pressure of time speeds up the process of memorizing.

- *Time to allow: 1 minute a day*
- *How to go about it*

  - ✓ Set the timer at one minute. Write down as many positive qualities as you can. Compliments are also allowed.
  - ✓ It does not have to look good. Abbreviate words or phrases if you like.
  - ✓ Count the number of qualities afterwards.
  - ✓ Add newly discovered qualities to your positive list.
  - ✓ Your goal each week is to write down more qualities than the previous week.

Date	Number of qualities

Exercise 4.5: Rating the credibility of your new core belief

Reflect on the steps you have already taken and how this has affected your self-esteem.

* *Time to allow: 2 minutes*
* *How to go about it*

✓ Copy the positive statement you wrote in **Exercise 2.2 (page 39)**.

✓ Indicate with a cross how convinced you are of your new core belief.

My new positive core belief:

....

Date:

Credibility:

:——:——:——:——:——:——:——:——:——:——:

0   10   20   30   40   50   60   70   80   90   100

0 = not at all credible   100 = highly credible

5
Negative mind talk

In the previous chapter, you made the connection between the events recorded in your data log and positive qualities. This resulted in a list of positive qualities describing the kind of person you are. You will, no doubt, have experienced some doubts and reservations – there's always something to find fault with!

In this chapter, you will see how the old negative core belief keeps popping up in the form of 'negative mind talk'. You will also read how to keep this negative mind talk at bay.

5

'You excel at brushing praise aside', says Kevin. Luckily, after six weeks of positive data logging, Lindsey is a little more thick-skinned. And he is right: she is really good at it. How often has she heard herself say: 'Oh, it isn't a big deal really, you could do it too', when someone compliments her for the cake or biscuits she has made. And if someone says that her dog Daisy is very obedient, she attributes it to the 'easy-going' breed, which is downright nonsense. She has spent a lot of time training Daisy. Silly habit – the brushing aside has to stop ...

Beaver or woodworm

You have been working on your positive data log and are now able to look at yourself from a positive angle. Have you noticed how the foundations of your positive core belief are becoming stronger?

However, you also will have noticed a voice in your head regularly trying to subvert the positive experiences. This voice censors your positive assessment in the shape of, 'yeah, but ...'. After the 'but' comes an objection that turns the positive into a negative. Sometimes, the voice will work like a family of beavers – woodchips flying all over the place and trees being felled. Sometimes, the voice acts like a woodworm – secretly burrowing little holes. These will eventually also pulverize a strong construction. Beaver or woodworm, the outcome with both is that positive information is unable to prevail. This undermines building your positive core belief and therefore provides all the more reason to stop the negative mind talk.

What is negative mind talk?

Negative mind talk, or 'yeah-butting', stops positive information being processed. When building up your positive core belief, you need as much positive information about yourself as possible. But that is easier said than done, because there is always a 'yeah, but...' ready to pounce.

- When recording events in your positive data log, negative mind talk whispers in your ear that it's a waste of time, that you are an idiot if you feel any pride in doing it. Or, more subtly, that it is so-so, but that it could have been done faster or better.
- When thinking about positive qualities, your negative mind talk can interfere. You don't write down qualities you think of because it tells you that those qualities, such as assertiveness, aren't at all positive. Or your negative mind talk tells you that although you do stand up for yourself every now and then, it's only with people that like you anyway.
- When you copy the positive qualities from your positive data log to your positive qualities list, your negative mind talk gets a third chance. 'To qualify for the list, the quality (being honest, for instance) must be there 100 per cent of the time. And yesterday you used an excuse, so you are not honest ...'.

'But that's normal' is Denise's motto. At first she didn't really notice, but now that she has been writing in her positive data log for two months, she catches herself often thinking of words or phrases like 'normal', 'usual', and 'matter of course'. Gizem pointed it out to her a couple of times, which did help,

and since then Denise has been quick to recognize it and is
better able to prevent it. The other day, when they tried to
think of positive qualities together for the first time, negative
mind talk reared its ugly head again, however. Half the
qualities Gizem suggested were quashed by her negative mind
talk as 'nothing special'. The inner voice said the other half
represented 'nothing much, anyway'. Denise looks up to the
other mothers at school who have interesting jobs. They
always know what to say and know exactly what they want.
They do most of the talking at parents' evenings, although you
hardly ever see them helping out with practical matters.
'Maybe you should value helping with these practical matters
more', Gizem suggested, 'because that is your forte. And don't
pretend "everyone does it", because that is just not true!'

5 Why do you excel at negative mind talk?

The culprit, of course, is your negative core belief. It is still there and
will remain active for now, sending information in the wrong direction.
Through selective perception and selective memory, negative issues
are perceived more readily than positive ones. You notice small
negative details immediately whereas big positive deeds are over-
looked in an instant.

Cognitive dissonance also plays a part. This specialist term
describes a psychological phenomenon that affects everyone. If we
receive information that is the opposite of our convictions, we
immediately feel uncomfortable. If you have low self-esteem, you
won't be comfortable with positive information such as praise from
others or an entry in your positive data log. You notice it in your body
too sometimes, as you may become tense and start to shift in your
chair. It does not sit well with you and does not feel right.

We all have a natural tendency to diminish such contradiction,
which can be done in several ways. For instance, you may absorb only

the part of the information that fits with your convictions, or you may distort contradictory information in such a way it will fit. If you diminish your achievements, for instance by building up those who helped you, everything feels better and familiar. I bet you are an expert in finding downsides to any achievement too.

> Although Emma's positive qualities list includes 64 qualities, she still feels tense when reading them. There are qualities, however, that are no longer affected by negative mind talk; for example, she no longer has doubts about her work-related strengths. What a difference from three months ago when she replied to every one of Geri's suggestions with a sarcastic remark. Geri is persistent, that much has become clear. She ignores sarcasm and that works well. When Emma suggests that she is not always great or friendly, Geri responds: 'Who is?' Finally, Emma succeeds in not taking her 'second voice', as she calls her negative view of herself, too seriously. One day she wants to read through her list and conclude: 'I'm not too bad after all!'

Eight ways to put yourself down

You have considered a number of examples of negative mind talk above. All those 'yeah, buts' can be divided into several categories so that you can recognize them more easily.

- *It is normal.* You object that something is how it should be, that everyone does it, that it is part of your job. When you do so, you no longer see your behaviour as positive, but as neutral.
- *Compared with others ...* You constantly look at the accomplishments and qualities of others and try to compare yourself with them. Whereas you view others in a positive light, you see yourself from a negative one. Thus, you will always fall short.

- *Diminishing things*. You state that it's all relative, or you point out the negative aspects of what you did. This way you manage to diminish something that was in fact quite special and what you did well suddenly seems sloppy or dumb.
- *'Favourable' circumstances*. Basically, you dream up excuses for your positive deed or your good quality: it was very easy, you had help, you were in a good mood.
- *Higher demands*. You link something you did well directly to a higher expectation or demand: a demand in the future, for instance, or the need to apply your qualities in different fields. Your positive deed or quality is quickly forgotten about because you immediately focus on what it is you can't do yet.
- *It is not my doing*. You attribute positive deeds or qualities to others or to coincidence. This way they don't make your list of accomplishments. You do take credit for negative qualities, however!
- *The other side of the coin*. You look at a behaviour or quality from the opposite side and emphasize the downsides. You attach to these downsides greater importance and lose track entirely of the positive behaviour or quality: 'I am precise, but way too much so. This must be so annoying for my colleagues.'
- *Thinking positively about yourself is wrong*. You may view with disdain people who think or speak favourably about themselves. Praising yourself to the skies is just not done, you feel. These convictions can inhibit you when doing this book's exercises.

Negative mind talk is unwanted behaviour and is the reason why positive deeds don't make your positive data log. They are not recorded in your memory. When you do write a positive data log event, but think of a 'yeah, but...' and an objection to follow the 'but', chances are that it is processed in your memory as something negative, and so it is stored in the negative box in the archive.

In Exercise 5.1, you will be encouraged to make an inventory of the sort of negative mind talk you apply.

Getting started

The negative mind talk in your head is a tough cookie that has been calling the shots for a long time. Adding 'yeah, but ...' to something positive is such an automatic thing, you hardly ever notice you're doing it. Your buddy or someone else you are close to can help you become aware of it. They can point it out, for instance, by raising their finger at every 'yeah, but ...', or telling you: 'that's negative mind talk again'. You can agree on a certain sentence or gesture. You can also agree on them using a nonsense word as a signal, such as 'Eskimo' or 'Sesame Street'.

When Paul hears Agnieszka run her positive deeds into the ground, he starts humming a particular tune. He has explained that he will do so every time he hears 'yeah, but ...'. Agnieszka doesn't usually realize she's engaging in negative mind talk, and when he starts humming louder and louder, she interrupts her story to ask what is wrong. When she realizes, she hums along with him and they both burst out laughing.

Lindsey and Kevin have agreed that when they are in company, he will signal with a quiet cough that she has missed a compliment.

When it is clear to you how and when negative mind talk functions, you won't need your buddy's signals any more. You will recognize it yourself and be able to correct it. Getting rid of it entirely is the goal, but that is easier said than done. Negative mind talk will linger around for some time to come. 'I am caring because I called my dad', you write in your positive data log, 'but I should have talked to him sooner', you think immediately afterwards and the event already feels much less positive.

You can learn to react in a different way. 'Be gone', you might think and ignore your negative mind talk, or re-run your initial positive view of an event and leave out the 'yeah, but ...' part: 'I am caring because I called my dad. That's it.' Another way is to replace 'but' with 'and'. 'I am caring because I called my dad *and* I could have talked to him sooner.' Chances of the negativity doing its work are higher in the latter case. Exercise 5.1 will help you to overcome your negative mind talk.

Five ways to negate compliments

Even when being praised, your negative mind talk will try to intervene. When someone else shows their appreciation of you, you feel the need to correct them because it doesn't feel quite right to you. When someone compliments you on a piece of clothing, for instance, you remark that it is very old, that you got it from your sister who had finished with it, that you bought it in a sale, or picked it up in a charity shop. Everyone has their own methods, but in all cases it comes down to praise being blocked and not being stored in your memory. In short: it was a missed opportunity to help build up your positive core belief.

- *Blocking out compliments.* You do not hear a compliment and your reaction will suggest the message was not received. The person who paid you the compliment will be confused: 'Did they hear what I said or not?'
- *Brushing compliments aside.* You register a compliment, but find it difficult to process the positive message. You talk around it or pay the other person a compliment too.
- *Not believing a compliment.* You react with disbelief or even indignation: 'Whatever makes you think that?' Or, 'What on earth are you talking about?' The person who paid you the compliment might get the feeling they are being rebuked.

- *Knowing better*. You correct the other person: 'There isn't that much to it', or 'You don't quite see that the right way', or even 'You must be mad!' The person paying the compliment gets the feeling they are being criticized.
- *Looking for a hidden meaning*. Your immediate reaction to a compliment is, 'do they want something from me?' You are distrusting and think the person complimenting you wants you to do something.

When praising others and paying attention to how the compliment is received, you will notice the effect it has on you when praise is not accepted. This will help you to accept compliments given to you.

Agnieszka has cooked a meal. 'Nothing special really', she tells Paul, 'just a quick bite to eat'. 'That was delicious', says Paul, 'I love it when you cook'. He waits for more negative mind talk, and yep, there it is: 'Shame that the pasta was overdone'. Typical Agnieszka, she's always ready to criticize herself. Paul hums his negative mind talk tune and Agnieszka has to laugh. The message gets through. 'But that pasta really wasn't al dente', she has to add.

She tells Paul how she had worked with her head of department yesterday and how he paid her a compliment. 'My initial reaction always is that it was just normal and that anyone else could have done it too. And then I start finding fault with what I did. I always manage to find something that wasn't quite right, or could have been better. It is exactly what my mum used to do. If I scored an eight, I had not worked to the best of my abilities. And if I scored a nine, it could be a ten next time. I'm fed up with all that.' Paul has noticed numerous examples of this over the past few weeks. Sat down together, they are easily able to draw up a long list of qualities. Agnieszka has trouble sleeping that night.

Receiving a compliment is in fact a very easy thing to do. Listening attentively to the other person, looking them in the eyes, and letting them finish what they are saying is the first step. The next step is not to dismiss the compliment immediately, instead allowing the message to sink in. Then, after a short moment that makes clear that you are indeed accepting the compliment, say: 'thank you' or 'it is good to hear that'. And as a final step record the compliment in your positive data log as soon as possible. Exercise 5.2 will help you do this.

Persisting and continuing

It is best to keep your positive data log for six months or so, and the same goes for adding qualities to your positive qualities list. I also advise you to do the one-minute exercise on a regular basis (Exercise 5.3, see pp. 86–7). The facts you collect form the basis of your new positive core belief, and the meanings you attach to those concrete events in your positive data log are the connections between the various elements. You have probably already noticed that your mood improves when you reflect on positive issues and that you become more active and have more courage to take new steps. By keeping the positive data log and updating the positive qualities list for the next few months, your mood will improve even further.

Your negative mind talk will also demand your attention. Even if you think you have got rid of it, it will pop up again from time to time. Realize that you will need to repeat things every now and then – if the exercises work for you now, they will be easier to repeat in the future.

Exercises

Exercise 5.1: Making an inventory of your negative mind talk

Your negative mind talk is trying to undermine you. The effort you put into discovering positive qualities will have been for nothing if you link them with something negative. It will even reinforce your low self-esteem.

* *Time to allow: 35 minutes*
* *How to go about it*

  ✓ Which of the eight forms of negative mind talk do you recognize?
  ✓ Add your own examples to the list.
  ✓ When you detect negative mind talk, re-run your initial positive view of that event leaving out the 'yeah, but ...' part.
  ✓ Agree with your buddy how they will signal you are engaging in negative mind talk.

Eight ways to put yourself down

It is normal
* ...., but that is normal.
* ...., but surely everyone would have done that.
* ...., but it is my job.

Compared with others ...
* ...., but others can do it better.
* ...., but I am hardly as ... as ...

Diminishing things
* ...., but that is so inconsequential.
* ...., but I don't always do that, I'm not always like that.
* ...., but it took a lot of effort.

Favourable circumstances
* ...., but it was an easy exercise.
* ...., but I was helped.

Higher demands
* ...., but it can be done much better.
* ...., but from now on, I always have to do it like this.

It is not my doing
* ...., but that is simply what I was taught at home.
* ...., but I just got lucky.

The other side of the coin
* ...., but if I do so, I disappoint people.
* ...., but it is the easiest way out.

Negative associations
* ...., but you can't say that about yourself.
* ...., you are such a brag!

Own examples
* ...., but ...
* ...., but ...
* ...., but ...

My buddy will signal me engaging in negative mind talk with a:
* Gesture: ....
* Sentence: ....
* Nonsense word: ....

Exercise 5.2: Receiving compliments
Receiving and accepting compliments is an art that can be learned.
The recipe? Practise a lot.

- *Time to allow: 2 minutes a day*
- *How to go about it*

  ✓ From now on, do not dismiss compliments others pay you, but embrace them.

  ✓ Enter below, or in your positive data log, which compliments you received and what your response was.

Compliment diary

Date + time	Compliment	Received from whom?	My response: dismissed it/ accepted it

Exercise 5.3: The positive data log, the one-minute exercise, and the positive qualities list

The positive data log is still part of the programme. If you are successful in dismissing negative mind talk, this should lead to an increase in the number of positive data log entries and positive qualities.

*   *Time to allow: 30 minutes a day*
*   *How to go about it*

    ✔ Write in your positive data log on a daily basis.
    ✔ Pay extra attention to compliments you receive in the next few weeks and make a note every time you managed to bring the negative mind talk to a halt.
    ✔ Think of qualities for the positive data log events.
    ✔ Repeat the one-minute exercise on a regular basis.
    ✔ Add newly discovered qualities from the positive data log and one-minute exercise to your positive qualities list.
    ✔ Re-read the positive data log and the positive qualities list on a regular basis.

Example: A page from Denise's positive data log

Date + time	Positive data log event	Feeling	Meaning
3 February	Compliment: The teacher said I am really good at checking for lice	happy	patient kind
3 February	I did not dismiss the compliment	satisfied	
5 February	I have joined a group of mums at the school playground	proud	courageous

5

Date + time	Positive data log event	Feeling	Meaning
9 February	Compliment: Gizem said I was creative. I said 'there wasn't much to it'. Then I realized that was negative mind talk and said so too.	satisfied	creative I try my best

Exercise 5.4: Rating the credibility of your new core belief

Reflect on the steps you have already taken and how they affect your self-esteem.

* *Time to allow: 2 minutes*
* *How to go about it*

    ✓ Copy the positive statement you wrote in **Exercise 2.2 (page 39)**.
    ✓ Indicate with a cross how convinced you are of your new core belief.

My new positive core belief:

....

Date:
Credibility:

:——:——:——:——:——:——:——:——:——:——:

0   10   20   30   40   50   60   70   80   90   100

0 = not credible at all   100 = highly credible

6
Changing your behaviour

The previous chapter dealt with the negative mind talk that your negative core belief bombards you with. You first learned to recognize your negative mind talk and then to ignore it or to silence it. If you are successful in doing this, you 'save' the experiences you are satisfied with or are proud of. It improves your mood and gives you more energy. Changes in your behaviour will come spontaneously.

You can also take the initiative and change your behaviour – the focus of this chapter. You research your old ways. You decide which behaviour is more befitting of your new positive view of yourself, and this is how you will try to behave in the future. If you start behaving differently, you gain other, positive experiences. This not only improves your mood, it also strengthens your new behaviour, your self-esteem, and confidence.

6

'I have to do it differently this time', Steve thinks. He has felt inferior since puberty. He was very tall for his age and was bullied about it. He sought to hide his height by stooping, by making himself invisible in class, and avoiding extracurricular activities. 'I don't want to slink off with my tail between my legs again after just a year.' Together with his ex Helen (despite their divorce, she is still supportive of him), he thinks of what he can do differently in his new job. He has to stick with it, that much is clear, but how can he do that? Making contact with colleagues seems important to him: chatting to them about work, but also about personal things and getting to know them a bit better. When he was anxious in previous jobs and doubted himself, he avoided contact with others. He kept plodding on alone, so that interacting with others became an even bigger problem, or so it seemed to him. He also wants to practise walking upright. Helen also suggests he ask others for advice if something is bothering him. In the past, he kept everything to himself, because he was scared of being found wanting. He was never supported at home, his mum and dad hardly showed interest in him, let alone his elder brothers. 'Fight your own battles' was the message. And if you didn't do so correctly, you were brought down a peg or two.

Survival strategies

Everyone learns something about themselves from the reactions of others. If, like Steve, you received little attention as a child, were criticized and hardly ever appreciated, chances are that you will develop low self-esteem. 'I am a good for nothing', Steve concluded early on, although he wasn't able to articulate it until much later. The attitudes of his father, mother, and two brothers, who were hard to approach and always critical of him, influenced Steve's view of others. Due to selective perception and selective memory, he reached a point where he could only see others as sources of criticism.

Although you will be unaware of it, such experiences provide you with rules on how to behave. 'Do not ask for help; you will be rejected anyway. So, take care of yourself', has become Steve's motto. 'Get out before you are found out', is another. He started behaving accordingly and still lives this way. It is his strategy to prevent criticism and rejection and keep unpleasant emotions and negative conclusions to a minimum.

In the long term, these behaviour patterns reinforce your negative core belief and a pessimistic view of others. It is a self-fulfilling prophecy. If you do not ask for help, it is likely you won't receive any and neither will you identify the people who are willing to help. And if you quit your job before you are found out, you'll miss out not just on negative feedback but on positive feedback as well. Furthermore, you'll miss the chance of learning more and becoming better at your trade.

Many people with low self-esteem stay in the background from an early age and do not take the initiative. Or instead they focus on hard work and perfectionism. They do all kinds of things so as not to fail and be rejected. Once you are on that track, it's not that easy to get off – but it can be done.

> Bryony seems to be an ideal employee, colleague, daughter, sister, niece, friend, and neighbour. She is good at registering others' wishes and needs and aims to please others all the time. She adapts easily and never refuses or ignores a request. She rarely asks anything of other people and has no demands of her own. 'And by the way', she says, 'I have no identity either'. Of late, she has given this a lot of thought. She gets sad because she only sees herself as someone who sacrifices herself for others. 'I am like a chameleon', she concludes with regret.

Ridding yourself of your old behaviour patterns

6

You may have never considered the fact that many behaviour patterns are acquired, instead putting everything down to your personality, which is a given. Changing your behaviour patterns is, however, possible and vitally important if you want to see yourself in a different light. 'Feelings follow behaviour' – this means you have to show behaviour that befits your new core belief to enhance your self-esteem and confidence. Even if it is only a first step and does not feel like your 'own' yet, it will help you to strengthen your faith in that new core belief and you will gradually start feeling better within yourself. And feeling better makes it easier to take the next step.

> 'I am somebody' was the new sentence Bryony chose. Later on she amended it to 'It is okay for me to be who I am'. After eight weeks of positive data logging, she has started to believe in it.
>
> At work, she has started taking things a little easier, which has not led to her dismissal. On the contrary, her boss has sent

her home early a couple of times. He said she had been working so hard lately and that she ought to take some time off for herself. A colleague complimented her because she was much less stressed. 'Taking it a bit easier at work is something that I want to continue doing', she tells Bibi. 'Though I don't fancy doing that in my private life!'

Yet she is annoyed at herself sometimes, because she checks up on everyone. 'What would it be like if I were convinced that I am okay?', she wonders. 'Maybe I would become less sensitive. I guess I would be less afraid to say no and I wouldn't apologize all the time.'

It can be hard to determine which behaviour patterns are part of your survival strategy and which are your 'rules for living' that control your behaviour to this day. Look out for the following signals:

- *Behaviour determined by fear*. If you become tense at the thought of doing something differently for a change, if you fear being rejected or being found out, this behaviour is probably part of your old 'rules for living'.
- *Being shackled*. Behaviours that you display often, but which also make you feel you are shackled, may once have been a survival strategy. Do you ever get the feeling you want to break free?
- *Others' remarks*. If you listen to the advice and criticism of people close to you, this will help you gain a better understanding of your behaviour patterns.
- *Feeling envious*. Are you envious of people doing what you secretly dream of? That could signal you are stuck on a strict 'rule for living'.

Exercise 6.1 will help you research behaviour patterns that go hand in hand with your rules for living dictated by your negative core belief.

Michael isn't finding it easy to identify what he wants to do differently. During his next performance interview, he would like to bring up the matter of promotion. That would be something new for him and he would also like to ask for a pay rise. Gaining promotion is not something he has ever strived for because he's been afraid he wouldn't live up to it. He likes to err on the safe side in his job as a branch manager of a travel agency.

When stretching before a run, he talks to Karim, who he asked to be his buddy after hesitating about doing so for a long time. Although Karim is someone who likes big gestures, he knows how to nuance things: 'Start small', he says, 'that way you can't go wrong'. Michael would actually like to take on more of a challenge. He is always careful, always does as he is told. But he never comes up with initiatives or proposals himself. He does see possibilities though. In branch manager meetings, people are often asked to work out a plan, for instance. He feels he could do that, as he does have ideas, it's just that he doesn't share them with anyone. Karim gives him a high five. 'Now let's go running.'

New behaviours

If you have a clear picture of your old rules and behaviour patterns, those that best fit your new core belief will, usually, be the exact opposite. For Steve, this means walking upright instead of stooping down, staying on instead of quitting, and asking for help instead of plodding on alone. Bryony wants to be able to say 'no' instead of always meeting other people's expectations. She also wants to 'keep more in touch with her own feelings', although she has no idea yet what her wishes and desires are.

Being self-effacing may reflect low self-esteem ('I am worthless'), but it doesn't communicate a new positive view of yourself such as 'I am worth something'. Taking your own wishes and boundaries seriously fits better with your new conviction. Feeling like a 'nobody' may make you appear invisible, but feeling 'I am someone' will make you want to be seen.

Things you hadn't considered previously suddenly emerge together with your new core belief. Because you start looking at yourself differently, you see qualities and skills you had not imagined you had. Maybe you even fantasize about expanding your knowledge or taking a different turn in life. You can give your fantasy free rein in Exercise 6.2 when you think of which behaviour befits your new positive core belief. Would you like to behave differently at work? Would you like to become less of a perfectionist, delegate more or be more in the foreground? Would you like to deal differently with your family or your kids? Maybe you would like to say 'no' more often and apologize less. Or maybe you would just like to share more personal experiences with your friends. You might even like to dress differently or change something about the way you look. You could also think about changing your circumstances. You could hang out more often with people who support you, for instance, and avoid situations or relations that cause you stress.

Getting started

You do not have to wait until your new positive core belief is complete – you can start now. And you do not have to make radical changes, as it is best to start small; the idea is to experiment with new behaviour and gain new experiences.

As a first step, determine whether you already display the behaviour you have chosen spontaneously. Looked at from the right angle and paying attention to small details, you will be surprised by how often you already show the desired behaviour. Learning something new is easier when you reflect on what is (already) going well, so write it down in your positive data log with an exclamation mark or smiley face in the margin!

Then, you can make plans to display the chosen behaviour more often. Think of circumstances in which you dare to behave according to your new rules. With practice, it will come naturally and feel more like the real you. If you like it and would like to continue with it, plan to take a more difficult step. No giant leaps though – tiny steps will do.

6

Lindsey wants to rid herself of her 'invisibility'. As a reaction to bullying in primary school, she tried to behave as inconspicuously as possible, though she made a huge effort with the few friends she did have. She paid a great deal of attention to their wishes and asked little in return. It was always about their problems, never hers. Although she is no longer being bullied, things are much the same. She only talks about her own feelings with her husband. She always shows interest in her friends and she is always willing to listen. This way she never has to commit herself. This may appear a safe way to act, but sometimes it goes wrong – then she feels a 'nobody'. She would like to be a little more forward. She would love to participate more in conversation and become more personal, just like her friends.

Before her illness, she tried to avoid contact with people at work. If there was a team lunch, she never joined in the conversation. Lately, however, she has joined her colleagues for lunch more often and begun to chat, which hasn't gone too badly. Next week, she is to start working more hours and she has decided to go to the departmental meeting. No doubt she'll be asked about her absence from work. 'Maybe I can open up about that', she thinks. 'I won't give too many details, but just tell them honestly that I was overstressed.' She decides she should make a fresh start.

Three weeks later, Lindsey has answered quite a lot of questions and tried not to keep her distance. She has told people about what has been going on, and expressed that she is happy to be back. They were not surprised at all. A couple of colleagues she had little contact with before she became ill were very warm and supportive. Each afternoon when she gets back from work, she writes in her positive data log as she feels pride or satisfaction.

Persisting and continuing

Whatever you decide on, it will take time for the new behaviour to become familiar. If you have a natural ability for picking up others' signals, like Bryony, taking your own wishes into account will be quite a challenge. Maybe you don't know what your own needs are and thus you might, without thinking about it, offer your services again without realizing it. It is therefore very important to reward yourself in the positive data log for every small step forward. Once you have made a start, the new behaviour will become easier and more familiar because it is clear that you benefit from it.

Such a process of change is hardly ever smooth. Especially if you are stressed or have a setback, the old negative core belief can regain control. You may also be scared off by your family's, friends' or colleagues' reactions. Family members who take it for granted that you are always there for them might protest if you say 'no' for once. Your boss might be disappointed if you stop working late every day. It is usual for such anger and disappointment not to be expressed openly but if it is, you can explain why it is important you take better care of yourself. Family, friends, and colleagues can also react positively, so don't be surprised if they praise you for your new approach. And, of course, these compliments belong in the positive data log.

You do not have to cut out the old behaviour entirely, either now or in the future. It is not a matter of all or nothing. You don't have to say 'no' to every request; you can take others into account and help them as well as doing your work precisely and fighting your own battles. It is a matter of ridding yourself of the excesses – keep what is good about your old ways, but develop another side too. The idea is for you to have a choice, not just obligations.

Michael has kept his word. He has joined a committee and has been to three meetings already. 'Thinking along is no problem and I also have a vision', he tells Karim, 'but I'm finding it difficult presenting that vision'. Keeping quiet is second nature to him and Michael thinks he knows why that is. When he was seven years old, his sister Liz was seriously ill. For four years, the family feared that she would die. Michael was unable to take it all in, though he did understand that he shouldn't bother his parents, so he kept quiet and he has been keeping quiet ever since. He has to fight that habit now. Although lately he has been sharing his ideas, he is very tired after the meetings. He cannot change overnight. It does give him comfort though that he understands why he is this way.

6

Exercises

Exercise 6.1: Creating an overview of your behaviour patterns

People with low self-esteem develop strategies early in life to avert the painful emotions that go hand in hand with their negative view of themselves. These emotions result in a set of 'rules for living' that still control their lives today.

- *Time to allow: 60 minutes*
- *How to go about it*

  ✓ Draw up a list of behaviour patterns that have been dictated by your negative core belief.
  ✓ Ask a buddy to help you with this.

My 'old' behaviour patterns:

....
....
....
....
....
....
....
....
....

Exercise 6.2: Developing new behaviour patterns

Develop behaviour that goes against your old rules and strengthens your new core belief. Behavioural changes are far more persuasive than changes of view or thinking.

- *Time to allow: 60 minutes*
- *How to go about it*

✓ Write down which aspects of your behaviour you want to develop or strengthen.
✓ Choose which behaviour you wish to focus on first.
✓ Don't change anything yet. First, pay attention to when you already display the behaviour spontaneously. Note this down in your positive data log.
✓ Next, plan how to expand on this behaviour. Describe the behaviour as well as you can and think of examples.
✓ Praise yourself for every step in the right direction.

'New' behaviours that befit my new positive core belief:

....
....
....
....
....
....

6

For now I wish to focus on:

....

For now I want to do this more/less:

....

Exercise 6.3: The positive data log, the one-minute exercise, and the positive qualities list

The positive data log is still part of the programme. If you experiment with new behaviour, you can reinforce yourself in the positive data log. While behaving differently, you will discover new skills and talents. You should add them to your positive qualities list.

* *Time to allow: 30 minutes a day*
* *How to go about it*

✓ Write in your positive data log on a daily basis.

✓ Pay extra attention to new behaviour you wish to develop and strengthen. Lower your standards and reinforce every small step in the right direction.

✓ Think of positive qualities for your data log events.

✓ Repeat the one-minute exercise on a regular basis.

✓ Add newly discovered qualities from the positive data log and one-minute exercise to your positive qualities list.

✓ Re-read the positive data log and the positive qualities list on a regular basis.

Example: Steve's notes

Date + time	Positive data log event	Feeling	Meaning
20 April	Told two colleagues that I dread crafts day	relieved	not afraid to show weakness
	Walked upright	satisfied	I am changing
20 April	Asked Mia whether I can consult her about a pupil	satisfied	not afraid to show weakness sensible

Exercise 6.4: Rating the credibility of your new core belief

Reflect on the steps you have already taken and how they affect your self-esteem.

• *Time to allow: 2 minutes*

• *How to go about it*

✓ Copy the positive statement you wrote in **Exercise 2.2 (page 39)**.

✓ Indicate with a cross how convinced you are of your new core belief.

My new positive core belief:

Date:
Credibility:

:——:——:——:——:——:——:——:——:——:——:

0   10   20   30   40   50   60   70   80   90   100

0 = not credible at all   100 = highly credible

6

7
Dealing with criticism

New behaviour was the theme of the previous chapter. You were shown how to exchange your old behaviour patterns for behaviour that befits your new positive view of yourself. When you behave differently, your environment reacts differently too. In most cases, this has favourable results and your new behaviour and self-esteem will be strengthened further.

Criticism by others can remain a sensitive issue for some time. It arouses the old negative core belief, making you feel worthless again. In this chapter, you will learn to deal with criticism better and not to be totally shaken up by it.

7

> Michael rarely receives criticism. In fact, he does everything to prevent it. He is friendly, helpful and he prefers to listen rather than speak so that no one can find fault with him. At parties, people can always ask him to hand out food and drinks or help with the dishes. At least that way he doesn't have to converse much and run the risk of not knowing what to say.
>
> Steve, in contrast, has received criticism all his life. When he reflects on his jobs, he breaks out in a cold sweat. He can remember every detail of painful remarks made during meetings at work. He's rarely made it to a performance review, because he leaves before it's due. He now realizes he listened selectively back then – he viewed all his colleagues' comments in a negative way. And this was no different in his private life – friends only had to raise an eyebrow for him to conclude that they were disapproving of him.

Criticism is deadly if you take everything at face value

When you have low self-esteem, you interpret others' remarks negatively even when no criticism was intended, and you feel you are being judged when asked a question. A vague remark, a certain look, the fact that someone does not look you in the eye, each of these you interpret as disapproval. Even if you are being criticized, you take it much harder than intended. Your low self-esteem causes you to take a remark about one aspect of your behaviour as criticism of your entire being. Because your negative core belief emerges as soon as you receive criticism, it feels like a stab in the back and logically you react with strong emotions and worry a lot afterwards, sometimes for days on end.

To avoid confrontations and the attendant strong emotions, everyone develops their own strategy. The most common include the following:

* *Avoiding situations where you expect criticism.* These include calling in sick on the day of your performance review, postponing your oral exam, quitting your job, or ending your relationship immediately after your first row.
* *Preventing criticism by behaving impeccably.* You are meticulous in your preparation, are always ready to go, you ask nothing for yourself, and you certainly never criticize anyone yourself. Other ways to avoid criticism and rejection are: avoiding contact, avoiding standing out, and apologizing in advance.
* *Counterattacking.* You may keep criticism at bay by attacking others but this is only a short-term solution. Often you feel ashamed and are sorry afterwards and you start to think even more badly of yourself as a consequence.
* *Correcting any 'mistake' straightaway.* You may have been alerted to a 'mistake', but you feel like you can still make up for it, by taking it seriously and bettering your life. This softens the pain somewhat and you can cling on to the illusion that you have pleased the other person after all.

It is these strategies that you turn to automatically. You do this naturally, despite the long-term disadvantages. Perhaps you have run-ins with your colleagues because you criticize them before they can criticize you. Or maybe you feel you have to change all the time, because others point out flaws to you. The biggest disadvantage, of course, is that by avoiding criticism, you won't learn to deal with it better. And so you remain very sensitive to it. In Exercise 7.1, you will explore how to deal with criticism.

> 'Attack is the best form of defence' is Emma's motto. She often reacts fiercely to a colleague's proposal or suggestion. She didn't use to be like that. In the past, she held back and applauded others. Colleagues she has worked with for years have spotted the change and lately she has begun to acknowledge it too. She can react aggressively, especially when Jack acts like mister know-it-all. She must confess that it feels quite good to cut him down to size, but afterwards she regrets doing so. At home, she feels small and weak, and when she goes to bed after much worrying, she knows it'll take ages before she falls asleep. The following day is even worse, since she usually feels sad and rather unstable. She dreads work and would like to call in sick but she is better than that. From the way her colleagues look at her, she can tell that they have talked about her behind her back; she feels rejected.

From destructive to constructive

Nobody likes to be criticized, but it doesn't have to be a disaster. However bad it seems, it won't physically harm or kill you. Pay attention to how people who are satisfied with the way they are react to criticism. They may feel down for a while, but they will be much less affected than someone with low self-esteem, who is often devastated.

As long as your negative core belief and its attendant unfairness dominate, you will hear more criticism than is necessary. The selectiveness of your perception is the culprit. You start feeling sombre, sad or anxious. Also, when someone does criticize you, it is likely to be about something you shouldn't be doing, not about what you should be doing differently or better. You may feel cast adrift and become lethargic, it seems you can't do anything right.

You can help yourself in this regard, not by trying harder still, but by reducing the 'unfairness' of your perception. Try not to blow out of all proportion any criticism aimed at you. As your confidence grows, you will find this less difficult to do.

Steve has been teaching for five months now. He is being retrained as a primary school teacher and Mia, an older colleague, counsels him. He can ask her for advice and she talks him through how things are going, providing suggestions and advice. Steve has tended to see Mia as meddlesome rather than supportive but he is turning this around.

Today, they discussed two children in the class who regularly fight. Mia asked about the latest incident and how he handled the conflict. In the past, he would have taken such a question as implied criticism, but this morning he managed to think that it was 'just a question', nothing more. He also handles Mia's suggestions better. A suggestion no longer means he has 'got it wrong again'. When he recalls the conversation that evening, he feels less tense. Mia praised him for his approach and they had a brainstorming session together. It actually felt quite good to talk to her about how things are going in class.

Learning to listen to criticism

You don't have to be afraid of criticism – you can use it to your advantage and to better yourself. It will help you to consider criticism from a distance and not become over-emotional. Instead, ask yourself the following questions and consider your responses seriously.

- *Am I really being criticized?* By asking yourself this question you can postpone your emotional reaction for a while and you will be reminded that you often look at things negatively. Keep your answer to this question short: 'yes' or 'no'. If the answer is 'no', you can brush the remark aside (bin it!) and go on with what you were doing. If in doubt, this is a good rule to follow: only remarks that contain something negative about your behaviour in a literal sense are real criticism, the rest can be binned straightaway. When in doubt, ask the person who has criticized you: 'This sounds like criticism, was it meant that way?' True, others really ought to articulate criticism much more clearly. Only if your answer to this question is 'yes', ask yourself the following.

- *Do I agree with it?* By asking yourself this question, you can postpone your emotional reaction and may consider your opinion to be just as valid as that of the other person. Sometimes you will agree, sometimes not. Keep your answer short again: 'yes' or 'no'. If the answer is 'no', then the remark can go straight in the bin. Get rid of it! You don't have to provide reasons to defend or exonerate yourself. It's okay to disagree with someone and you should let them know: 'I hear what you say, but I'm afraid I don't share your opinion', for example. If the answer is 'yes, I agree', go straight to the following question. A third possibility is that you agree in part with what has been said, so ask yourself the following question in relation to that part only.

- *Do I want to change it?* Everyone has good qualities and strong points, but they also have downsides and weaknesses. That's part of life. By asking yourself 'do I want to change it?', you can keep your emotions at a distance. It also reminds you that it is perfectly okay to have a few quirks and weaknesses, even if others criticize you for them. Keep your answer short – 'yes' or 'no' – as you don't have to provide reasons or defend yourself. If the criticism is about a feature you don't want to change, then don't occupy yourself with it any longer – in the bin, gone! You could say to the other

7

person: 'I hear what you say and I agree'. Ask yourself the final question only if you do want to change some characteristic.

- *When and how do I want to change it?* By asking yourself 'when and how?', the urgent need to change no longer applies. You are reminded that even if you want to change certain behaviour patterns, you are free to choose when and how to do so. It may be wise to wait until a later date when you are less sombre or anxious, or more energetic and confident. Keep your answer short: 'yes' or 'no'. If you decide to live with your downsides for now, you don't have to bother with the 'how'. So, bin it! If you do want to change a certain behaviour pattern, then grab your diary. Decide when you want to start and note it down. Only when that date comes around do you work out how to do so, not before.
Exercise 7.2 will help you learn to listen to criticism without being shaken up by it.

When Michael is criticized, he winces and wishes the ground would swallow him up. His buddy Karim thinks that he should face criticism head on because, in his experience, it makes you stronger. 'You wouldn't believe how much criticism I received when I started up my company', says Karim. 'If I had cared then, I'd now be out of work.' Karim's pretty good at it himself, Michael thinks, he doesn't mince his words. Just last week he said I run like an old woman!

Michael tells Karim that his self-help book states that you should first determine whether what has been said is indeed criticism, then if it is decide whether you agree with it, and finally whether you want to change it. 'You don't have to be afraid of criticism – you can use it to your advantage and better yourself', says Michael, more to convince himself than Karim. 'I agree', says Karim. 'Some of the criticism I received really helped me. Sometimes, when you're on the wrong track, it's good to have someone point it out to you. But you have to be able to

7

differentiate, because if you take everything that is said to you seriously, you will never get things done.'

With his girlfriend Caroline, Michael likes to go over the details. He tells her today that Dunya, a new employee, had a go at him. She said she doesn't feel she's received adequate training and doesn't know who to turn to for advice. She complained that she always has to tidy her desk when she arrives in the morning, as her colleague who shares it leaves it in a mess. Caroline asks Michael, 'Why not ask yourself the four questions about this.' 'First: the mess on the desk. Is that criticism? Yes it is, but should you take it personally?' 'No', says Michael. 'Would you like to change something about it?', Caroline continues. 'No, that's going too far. Dunya can discuss it with her colleague herself', says Michael. Caroline exclaims, 'Bin!' and suggests moving on. Michael says he thinks the poor training is the main concern. 'Is that a criticism?', asks Caroline. 'Yes, it is, no two ways about it', replies Michael. 'Do you agree with it?', asks Caroline. 'Yes, I do', says Michael, 'she's right, she hasn't received very good training'. Just when Dunya started working there, Astrid became ill. All of a sudden they had to do without a full-time employee, who also happened to be the person responsible for training new members of staff. 'Do you want to do anything about it?', asks Caroline. 'Yes, Dunya needs proper training', says Michael. He will think about who he can assign to help train her, as he doesn't have the time to do so himself. 'See, it's not such a big thing being criticized, is it?', says Caroline. No, it's not such a big thing, but he sure is unaccustomed to it.

Getting started

All tasks are difficult before they become easy, and that is certainly true of trying to deal with criticism. Of course you would prefer not to receive any criticism at all – everybody does. The exercises in this chapter will help you fend off others' 'critical' remarks.

It takes practice to turn off the autopilot. It sees criticism in everything. People with low self-esteem feel they are criticized nearly all the time. Their standard reply to the first question, 'Is it really criticism?', is 'Yes, of course it is'. Another fault is to see others' criticism as 'the truth' – if only you were to do the same for praise! You skip the third question because it is only natural to change things you are dissatisfied with. The result is that you are already at work on the fourth question before you have listened to what was being said. If you really attend to the 'criticism' you receive, and take your time to ask and answer the four questions, much criticism will evaporate into thin air. Do not despair if you cannot always distance yourself from criticism, as there will be many other opportunities.

Emma finds the four questions allow her some space. Especially when she feels she might explode, the question 'Is it really criticism?' helps her keep her emotions in check. She has managed not to snap at Jack again, which is quite something.

She has trouble with the fact that she has to answer the questions with a single word, 'yes' or 'no' and she finds the question 'Do you agree with the criticism?' especially hard. Often she finds she agrees in part with what has been said, so her sister Geri offers a solution: 'Throw away what you disagree with, and only address what you do agree with', she says, 'then the criticism is smaller and you can handle it'. Emma likes this idea. 'Do you want to change it?' She rarely can answer that right away – and sometimes she does want to change something, but not everything. Take Jack's remarks about her willingness to help, for instance. 'Don't work yourself to the bone for guests who won't tip you anyway', Jack has told her repeatedly, 'you're like a puppet on a string'. Emma concludes that Jack's remarks are a criticism, especially because of the tone of voice he adopts, although, she thinks, 'he didn't actually say I'm doing anything wrong'.

Now for the second question, 'Do I agree?', that's a tough one for Emma. She thinks it part of her job to help guests who require information or need help. Even when put upon, you have to remain friendly and your attitude should not depend on tipping. 'I disagree, so it can go right in the bin', Emma says. On the other hand, she can be a bit too compliant at times. She has trouble with people who do not vacate their room on time on the day of departure, for instance. Jack deals with them rigorously and just sends the cleaners in. 'Partially agree', she thinks. 'And do I want to change that?', she ponders. To her own surprise she remains calm. Yes, she would like to be more forceful, but in a friendly way, of course. She would like to keep to the rules, especially at busy times. After all, there are knock-on effects when rooms are not vacated on time.

Persisting and continuing

A whole new world will open up for you when you learn to deal with criticism in this way. With each question, a part of the criticism is consigned to the bin. The only bit to address with the fourth question is the criticism you agree with, what you are taking to heart and wanting to change in the future. You have turned it into constructive criticism. Maybe a 'thank you' is in order to the person who delivered the remark. Anyway, you should definitely make a note in your positive data log that you reacted calmly.

Take care that you do not overburden yourself with new demands. If you did, you might automatically answer the question 'Do I want to change it?' 'yes', so be especially critical in your answer. Do not record more than two things you intend to change, as the rest can be tackled once these two have been resolved.

Exercises

Exercise 7.1: Trying to deal with criticism differently

Criticism is especially difficult to take for people with low self-esteem, which is why they develop strategies to avoid it. A first step towards change is awareness.

* *Time to allow: 10 minutes*
* *How to go about it*

  ✓ Complete the checklist below.
  ✓ Tick what applies to you or add to the list as appropriate.

Strategies to deal with criticism

* Avoiding situations in which I expect criticism.
* Preventing criticism by behaving impeccably.
* Counterattacking.
* Correcting any 'mistake' straightaway.
* ....
* ....

Exercise 7.2: A critical look at criticism

You can reduce the overall criticism by not accepting any message you receive as criticism. As a result, you become less sensitive to it.

* *Time to allow: 15 minutes a day*
* *How to go about it*

  ✓ Describe the criticism you receive in your diary.
  ✓ If you answer 'no' to one of the first three questions, throw the criticism (symbolically) in the bin.
  ✓ Continue with this until you notice that criticism no longer throws you off balance.
  ✓ Why not let a buddy help you?

Criticism diary

Date	
What was I criticized for, and who criticized me?	
Answer the four questions: 1. Am I really being criticized? 2. Do I agree with it? 3. Do I want to change it? 4. When and how?	yes / no yes / no yes / no
What have I done with the criticism?	

Exercise 7.3: The positive data log, the one-minute exercise, and the positive qualities list

The positive data log and the other exercises remain part of the programme.

- *Time to allow: 30 minutes a day*
- *How to go about it*

   ✓ Write in your positive data log on a daily basis.
   ✓ Pay special attention to dealing with criticism. Be aware of small steps in the right direction and do not ask too much of yourself.

✓ Think of positive qualities for your data log events. Be aware of putting yourself down.

✓ Repeat the one-minute exercise on a regular basis.

✓ Add newly discovered qualities to your positive qualities list.

✓ Re-read the positive qualities list and the positive data log on a regular basis.

Example: Michael's positive data log

Date + time	Positive data log event	Feeling	Meaning
27 March	Criticism from Karim ('you run like an old woman'). Did not really matter to me	proud	I can take a punch
30 March	Criticism from Dunya: was overwhelmed, but could think about it quietly later on. I was able to address this with Dunya	satisfied	I can take a punch finding solutions setting boundaries

Exercise 7.4: Rating the credibility of your new core belief

Reflect on the steps you have already taken and how they affect your self-esteem.

- *Time to allow: 2 minutes*
- *How to go about it*

   ✓ Copy the positive statement you wrote in **Exercise 2.2 (page 39)**.

   ✓ Indicate with a cross how convinced you are of your new core belief.

....

My new positive core belief:

....

Date:

Credibility:

:——:——:——:——:——:——:——:——:——:——:

0   10   20   30   40   50   60   70   80   90   100

0 = not credible at all   100 = highly credible

7

8
High demands and perfectionism

In the previous chapter, you were shown how to deal with criticism differently. By asking yourself the four questions presented there, you will have learned that a lot of criticism can go straight in the bin, which means you don't have to concern yourself with it. Do you agree with the criticism levelled at you by others? You can decide yourself if and when you want to change something. This makes criticism much easier to handle and you can use it to your advantage.

Many people with low self-esteem have learned to prevent criticism by doing things to the best of their ability. Setting high standards and trying to meet them is a laborious way to prevent criticism. This chapter is about perfectionism and what you can do about it.

8

> Lindsey has high standards regarding animal care. She walks her dog Daisy for 45 minutes three times a day. She also brushes the cats on a daily basis; if she fails to do this, she feels really guilty. Vacuuming the house every day is part of the deal too. She knows that a less strict regime is okay, but that is the voice of reason. Her feelings tell her something else, such as 'You have to ...', 'you may not ...', and 'it is not right to ...'. Until now, she has mostly acted on her feelings.

It can always be better

Not everyone with low self-esteem is a perfectionist. Perfectionism can be an answer to low self-esteem and the unpleasant negative feelings that go with it. If you strive for an A+ and are unable to settle for anything less, you are a perfectionist. There is nothing wrong with trying to do a job to the best of your ability. It can give you a feeling of satisfaction as well as extra energy. But your perfectionism may also result from a fear that you are not good enough. If that's the case, it will only drain your energy and you are unlikely to feel contented.

Perfectionism can appear in many guises: in your work (spending far too many hours preparing for a class), housekeeping (anxiously ensuring there is no clutter), your family and friends (always buying a large bouquet of flowers when you visit someone), your looks (never leaving the house without make-up). You do everything you can to prevent mistakes and being rejected, and you have learned that if you try very hard you can keep negative feelings at bay. Almost unnoticed, you keep raising the bar so that, eventually, you are ruled by hundreds of things you 'have to do', and you become 'shackled' by your perfectionism.

It soon became clear to Agnieszka, who is training as a nurse, what she should change about her behaviour – her perfectionism! She began to do so two months ago and, through trial and error, she has learned to keep it at bay somewhat. Sometimes she doesn't aim for an A+ in an exercise and is instead satisfied with a B. Then, quite suddenly, she loses sight of her new way of thinking and her autopilot tells her that even an A+ wasn't good enough. But she is getting better at it. She now makes time to chat to a patient, provide a quick hug or an encouraging word instead of focusing all her energy on 'the perfect report'. And to her own amazement, she is enjoying work more.

Who decides on the marks?

Perfectionists are very strong willed and set their standards very high. Although 6 out of 10 might be a pass for a particular piece of work, perfectionists will consider they have failed unless their mark is close to 10. If you are like that, you will rarely have reason to praise yourself.

Of course, there is nothing wrong with being attentive, being prepared, and making sure whatever you do is done with care. Indeed, these qualities belong on your positive qualities list, but if your perfectionism is a way to mask your low self-esteem, you will get your comeuppance sooner or later. You may think that by attending to the smallest detail in everything you do, the risk of failing, being criticized or rejected is diminished. But this strategy cannot work, as you can never meet the high standards you set for yourself and you will always be able to find fault.

Your selective perception ensures that small negative things are noticed and magnified, putting everything else in the dark. As a consequence, you conclude, 'I failed this time', which is often followed by, 'I'm a failure. I can't do anything right!' You may experience anger, fear or sadness, as well as hopelessness, which you find hard to deal with. Some people then quit altogether by becoming passive and inactive, whereas others are driven to do even better next time, so that their demands on themselves become even more severe. Increasingly, their perfectionism costs them more time and energy and they are rarely satisfied, which may result in depression or even a nervous breakdown. Although perfectionism results in some satisfaction when you achieve something major, it won't boost your confidence because you still believe the only way to avert criticism is to keep working yourself unrealistically hard. And you will never discover that people will appreciate your efforts even if the outcome is less than perfect.

Toning down your perfectionism can be achieved in two ways: by changing the way you judge yourself or by changing your behaviour – I would advise you to do both. To motivate yourself, you can list the advantages (benefits) and disadvantages (costs) of being a perfectionist in Exercise 8.1. Also think about what it would be like if you were to be a little less of a perfectionist.

Denise has often thought about helping to make the costumes for the annual Year 6 musical. She has never put her name forward before out of fear that she would not live up to others' expectations. The school is once again gearing up towards its end of year show and the subject has been chosen. The director has been picked, the roles have been cast, and parents and playground supervisors have been drafted in to help. People are needed to design and build the sets and to make the costumes but Denise is still in doubt. Gizem thinks that Denise should volunteer for costume making: 'This year you really should do it', she insists. 'You'll be good at it; they will be really pleased with you and it will be a bit of fun.' However, Denise has good reason to hesitate, as she hasn't done any for a while and may be out of practice. Is she really good enough?

Looking at things from a different angle

You can start to tackle your perfectionism by judging your actions, your qualities, and ultimately yourself less harshly. What you need to do is put your unrealistic grading system aside and start using normal grades. This means that you should praise yourself not only when you receive a 10, but also when you score an 8 or a 6. You need to realize that scores less than 10 are not a sign of failure, and that you also deserve a pat on the back for an 8 or a 6. Judging yourself less harshly also includes praising yourself for your effort and commitment, and not focusing solely on the end result. Perfectionists often do not take circumstances into account and there are no exceptions to the strict rules for them and no mitigating circumstances. Going to the gym on a Friday night deserves praise after a taxing week at work, even though you train less intensively than usual.

In the end, Denise did apply to make costumes despite being scared witless. Since the first meeting was held two months ago, Denise has felt uncomfortable and has contemplated not attending. Linda, who is a professional designer, is in charge

8

and made an inventory of everyone's capabilities. Denise is the only one who can draw patterns, while another couple of people are good with sewing machines. 'We don't need to make designer costumes', Linda assures them. 'The stage is far enough away that the audience won't be able to see every detail – the costumes don't need to be perfect.' Denise hadn't thought of that before and now she has turned Linda's sketches into patterns and they are all busy sewing.

'Think of what Linda has said', Denise says under her breath when she starts worrying again about the quality of her sewing. 'It does not have to be too precise. It is a play. Nobody notices the details.' That helps her to feel more positive about the costumes that she churns out. When the parents gather at Linda's workstation, they fit the finished clothes on mannequins and look at them – never up close, always from a distance. They congratulate each other on the results – 'They do look fantastic', Denise has to admit. Even though she still feels a little uncomfortable, she is certainly satisfied with the outcome.

Taking it easy for a while

Another means to pare down your perfectionism is to practise behaving opposite to the way you normally do. You could, for instance, consciously decide not to aim for 10 out of 10, but to settle for a 6 or 7 – and settle for 'good enough'. You do not have to make intentional mistakes and you do not have to throw your perfectionism out of the window entirely, as there is nothing wrong with doing things carefully or being attentive to others. Only rid yourself of that which you consider too extreme and unrealistic.

Perfectionists rarely, if ever, distinguish between important and unimportant issues. Their high standards apply any time, any place. Of course it is important that you avoid dropping a clanger, but in most cases it is okay if you are a little less precise or less attentive.

'A little less will do', is what I often tell my clients. It is important not to make spelling mistakes on an application from, for instance, but in an email to a friend it matters less. And if you would like to let your poorly aunt know that you are thinking of her, it matters more that you call her than how long the call lasts.

Lindsey's 'minimum programme' mostly affects Kevin and the animals. She sometimes skips combing the cat and on occasion only walks the dog for 30 instead of 45 minutes. 'I really do have to try and only do the minimum and only walk the dog for a quarter of an hour', she thinks, but then realizes that this is yet another demand. On Friday, she gets home tired from work and decides not to cook herself but to order a Chinese take-away. At the weekend, it is Kevin's turn to cook but he wants to go out for dinner and grab a movie afterwards. But that is just too much for Lindsey, 'dinner or a movie, but not both', she blurts out. She gives herself a shock, as she almost always accedes to Kevin's wishes. After all, he has to put up with her! It is odd to see that her refusal doesn't bother Kevin at all, and she gets better at doing a little less each week. On Monday, she leaves work early, while on Tuesday she takes the bus instead of walking. She skips the housework once, and gives a telesales person the brush-off when they call. Daisy has to manage with two half-hour walks and she gets Kevin to iron his own shirts. She is really starting to get the hang of it.

You can try out different behaviours with your 'minimum programme', and aim for a suitable pass mark instead of 10 out of 10. You can do this for all the different spheres of your life, including work (not working late for once), housekeeping (only iron what's necessary this week), and your family (having dinner together in front of the TV). Each time you experience a perfectionist demand, you can decide to give in or resist.

With such a programme you take the risk of being criticized or rejected, or even of being found out. The minimum programme that is explained in Exercise 8.2 is a way of finding out whether disaster is likely to strike. On the other hand, you also run the risk of discovering that a less perfectionist attitude does have advantages.

'I had never imagined myself seriously considering a minimum programme', thinks Bryony. 'It's good that my boss didn't know this when he hired me ...', although she has found that it is okay to take things a bit easier at work. Her boss hasn't been at all critical of her, in fact he told her to take the time owed to her, and they've had several relaxed conversations about new projects.

'But now the family ...', says Bibi. 'Do you think you dare to take that risk as well?' Bryony gets a tension headache at the thought of saying 'no' to her family, friends or neighbours, most especially her brother. Bibi tries to comfort her: 'You don't have to say no to everything'. She waits a moment and continues: 'Try not to be there for him right away all the time. Say for once that this week won't do, but next week will'. 'You're right', says Bryony, 'and I shouldn't always say I am sorry'.

Bryony's first victim is the guy with the charity box in front of the supermarket. She greets him and says she has already donated (which is true). She manages to swallow the 'sorry'. She acceded to her family members' requests before she realized she had, however, and over the past week she twice promised something without considering whether she actually wanted to do it. But she did brush off her niece with the argument 'you have much better taste than me' when Bryony was asked to go shopping with her to help choose a dress for a wedding. 'They can all manage very well without me', Bryony thought: 'I'm too busy, sorry, you know, deadlines ...', she blurted out. 'Little white lies', remarked Bibi, 'they're alright'.

Getting rid of dos and don'ts

The third way of addressing your perfectionism is also a behavioural change. The last exercise was very broad but this exercise focuses you on lowering a single demand. Perfectionism and high demands are closely connected, that much is clear. Many of these demands were likely passed on to you as parental rules or the rules of significant others. You took them for granted and now they have become your rules but you have never really considered whether you want to keep following them.

Agnieszka's head is buzzing with dos and don'ts. Her mother's ways are so much part of her life at present, it seems to Agnieszka that her mother is inside her head. But there are also demands of her own that she feels she has to abide by:

Dos:

- Be strong, persevere, do something about it, even when times are tough.
- Do everything to the best of your ability.
- A good education is what is most important.
- Be there for everyone.
- Dress nicely when visiting someone else.
- Cherish your family, there are so few of them.

Don'ts:

- Don't make mistakes.
- Don't cry or show your emotions.
- Don't whine, there are always people worse off than you.
- Don't stand out.

You can start developing your own rules by making an inventory in Exercise 8.3 of which dos ('You have to …') and don'ts ('You should not …') are still with you from your past. When you conduct your overview, you can decide which dos and don'ts you want rid of and which new self-chosen rules are to replace them. Start cautiously with a single do or don't. You can live according to the new rule for a while as a kind of experiment and, if you like it, you can continue, but you can always revert to the old behaviour if you wish. Agnieszka chose to lose the do, '*Be strong, persevere, do something about it, even when times are tough*'. After trying it out for two months, she decided that her new rule 'It is okay to ask for help' suits her better.

Getting started

Speaking of dos, there is a risk you might consider the above a new 'do'. Even if you feel that this chapter on perfectionism was written for you, that doesn't mean you should attempt immediate significant change – you should start small and cautiously, as large change is unnecessary. Small clues from your behaviour will tell you soon enough whether the risk of mistakes, criticism, and rejection is real, and you will learn what it feels like to let go and feel more positive about yourself.

You can go about this in a number of ways. You can consider practical exercises for yourself in advance, together with your buddy if you like, or you can focus on your intentions and keep your eyes and ears open for any opportunities that arise to practise. Just keep your data log close to hand and if you have disregarded a do or don't or if you have managed to resist high demands, those feats deserve to be mentioned in the positive data log (Exercise 8.4).

'Don't stand out, don't be annoying, and do everything you do perfectly': that was her father's advice when she was bullied at primary school. These dos and don'ts still determine Lindsey's life but she has decided to become more visible. When she started working again after her illness, she began joining her colleagues for lunch in the canteen. She joined in conversation every now and then and shared little bits of information about herself. Initially, she felt like she was intruding, but now she is very happy that she persisted. She is no longer taken aback when asked personal questions and feels more a part of the group, which she really likes.

Persisting and continuing

If you change something in your behaviour or attitude, it usually has an immediate effect. It's the same with perfectionism. Unfortunately, the short-term effects may be disappointing, as they are unlikely all to be positive. You may feel uncomfortable because things feel artificial, or anxious because you are scared of being rejected or abandoned. You may feel guilty because you have let others down, even if you know that this is not really the case; or you may be annoyed with yourself because you like your new attitude and wish that you had adopted it a long time ago.

You usually see the advantages much later. To convince yourself the wait is worthwhile, you need to know that no disaster will occur. New behaviour must be repeated to discover the favourable effects it has on you. Discover your new advantages and add them to the cost–benefit analysis in Exercise 8.1.

Denise undertook a cost–benefit analysis a while ago. She saw the advantages to settling for 'less than perfect': being less stressed and being easier on herself. She saw disadvantages too: letting others down, making mistakes, becoming sloppy and careless. 'The kids will probably think I'm not such a good mum', she told Gizem. 'No, and Aziz will want to divorce you', Gizem said, quickly adding that it was a joke when she saw Denise go pale. 'He might like it if you are less stressed.'

Being relaxed – she's still got some way to go. She is busy working on the costumes and her worktop is full of pieces of cloth, buttons, and reels of cotton. She tries to clear up before dinner, but doesn't always manage it. 'The kids have to entertain themselves a bit more', she tells Gizem. 'At first, I felt guilty about that. But I promised them they can dress up in the costumes on Saturday and now they love it. Aziz likes it too, because he can see that I'm in my element.'

In hindsight, Denise is happy she has decided to do everything a little less perfectly. 'And no designer wear', she has thought a hundred times before. She enjoys the costume group and discovers that she has other qualities as well. She knows she is able to develop her skills and has learned a lot from Linda. The kids and Aziz are not annoyed and even though the house is often a little less tidy, she is much happier. 'You really have something to live for again', Gizem concludes.

8

Exercises

Exercise 8.1: Attempting a cost–benefit analysis

If you want to work on your perfectionism, you need to become aware of the advantages and disadvantages of the way you have lived your life. It is also a good idea to imagine what the advantages and disadvantages are of behaving less perfectly.

- *Time to allow: 30 minutes*
- *How to go about it*
  - ✓ Enter the advantages and disadvantages of striving for perfection.
  - ✓ Enter the advantages and disadvantages of settling for less than perfect.
  - ✓ Draw a conclusion and describe your intention.

Cost–benefit analysis of perfectionism

	Advantages	Disadvantages
Striving for perfection		
Settling for less than perfect		

Conclusion: ....

I intend to: ....

Exercise 8.2: The minimum programme

You don't have to make mistakes to experiment with 'minimal' achievement.

- *Time to allow: 10 minutes a day*
- *How to go about it*

  ✓ Note circumstances in which you automatically place high demands on yourself.

  ✓ Decide each time whether you want to meet those demands or whether you are happy with a little less.

  ✓ Describe these successes below or in your positive data log.

  ✓ Draw a conclusion and describe your intention.

The minimum programme

Date + time	'Minimum' achievement

Conclusion: ....

I intend to: ....

Exercise 8.3: Getting rid of dos and don'ts

You can choose which of the demands, dos, and don'ts you have inherited and whether you want to keep them or get rid of them.

* *Time to allow: 30 minutes*
* *How to go about it*

  ✓ Note the dos and don'ts you have inherited.

  ✓ Indicate whether you want to keep them or not.

  ✓ Do not pick more than two to begin with.

  ✓ Go over the list again later and choose again.

Demands, dos, and don'ts

Demand, do, don't	Remove?
....	....
....	....
....	....
....	....
....	....
....	....
....	....
....	....

Conclusion: ....

I intend to get rid of the following do or don't:

....

....

Exercise 8.4: The positive data log, the one-minute exercise, and the positive qualities list

Making notes in your positive data log will help you address your perfectionism. The other exercises remain on the programme too.

* *Time to allow: 30 minutes a day*
* *How to go about it*

  ✓ Write in your positive data log on a daily basis.
  ✓ Pay special attention to perfectionism and diminishing your demands. Reward yourself in the positive data log for small steps in the right direction.
  ✓ Repeat the one-minute exercise.
  ✓ Add newly discovered qualities to your positive qualities list.
  ✓ Re-read the positive list and the positive data log on a regular basis.

8

Example: Agnieszka and Bryony's notes

Date + time	Positive data log event	Feeling	Meaning
4 June	Talked to a girl from my class about my fear of making mistakes (do: be strong, even when times are tough)	happy proud	I can overcome difficulties
26 June	Did not put money in charity collecting-box for a second time	happy	I can be assertive
27 June	Said 'no' to niece. She can go shopping with Aunt Dinah herself	satisfied	I can indicate boundaries

Exercise 8.5: Rating the credibility of your new core belief

Reflect on the steps you have already taken and how they affect your self-esteem.

* *Time to allow: 2 minutes*
* *How to go about it*

    ✓ Copy the positive statement you wrote in **Exercise 2.2 (page 39)**.
    ✓ Indicate with a cross how convinced you are of your new core belief.

My new positive core belief:

....

Date:

Credibility:

:——:——:——:——:——:——:——:——:——:——:

0   10   20   30   40   50   60   70   80   90   100

0 = not credible at all   100 = highly credible

9
The future

In the previous chapter, you had the opportunity to moderate your perfectionism. By experimenting with doing a little less, you can decide whether you want to continue making such high demands on yourself.

Although we are near the end of the book, it does not mean that you are now 'cured' of your low self-esteem. This chapter is about the future and how you can build on your achievements, how you can strengthen your self-esteem and confidence further, and how you can stop the old negative core belief from returning.

> Michael is still friendly but not so overly helpful any more. His buddy has challenged him to make more 'mistakes', which he has struggled to do. He does occasionally refuse to stand in for a colleague if asked to do so and is more assertive now. He has joined a project group and regularly voices his opinion there. 'They take me seriously. I hadn't expected that', he tells his girlfriend Caroline. The idea that he might be found out is still with him, but it isn't as strong any more.

Taking stock

Not everyone who reads this book will work through it in one go. Change occurs in stages. You might do your exercises for a couple of weeks until you experience some positive changes in your mood or behaviour and then stop for a bit. If you feel that you need more help, you can take the next step in your self-help programme. Use the book until you feel confident most of the time.

You first gathered facts in your positive data log that made you look at yourself from a different perspective – concrete behaviour, thoughts, and feelings you were positive about. Next you learned to interpret these facts in a positive way, which led you to identify the positive qualities that you possess. At the same time, you swapped old patterns of behaving for experimenting with new behaviour better befitting your new positive view of yourself. You really began filling the positive box in the archive, and started to feel comfortable with sayings such as 'I am okay', 'I am worthwhile', and 'I am somebody'.

It's time to finish the programme. In Exercise 9.1, you will be asked to write a summary of everything you have worked on until now. You will be describing what makes you a worthwhile person, which strong or special traits you possess, in which aspects of your life these are most visible, what you have achieved with your talents and how you have become the person you are now. You will be concluding your journey with this personal story.

Maybe you feel the need to mention your downsides too, to make the story complete. Previously, you were forbidden to do so because in the past negativity outshone the positives. Now you are more able to maintain a balanced view of yourself in which strong and weak points can co-exist.

'I was a scaredy-cat', Steve begins his story. 'At school I was bullied about my height, so I started stooping and avoided contact with people. Later, I avoided all difficult situations and became convinced that I was no good.' He starts making coffee and writes a title above the story: 'I can rely on myself', and picks up the thread again. 'Shame about all those years spent being sad', he writes, 'but they are not really lost years. I ran away a lot, but always started over again. I took on all kinds of things; I am a jack-of-all-trades. I am flexible and yet, I am a go-getter too.'

He pauses for a second cup of coffee. 'I am a good dad to my daughters. My children did not suffer as a result of my anxieties and they are secure in life.' Being a dad was often a good excuse not to work he thinks, but doesn't write that negative mind talk down.

'I have found the right kind of work for me. Being a teacher suits me and it is not too ambitious. I am good at working and dealing with children, have good organizational skills, and I am consistent and clear. I am calm and if there is a tense situation in class, I can clear the air with a joke. Those are good qualities. I don't have to feel inferior to my colleagues, although I am still receiving training. My assessments are good and I am well liked. So, I guess I can rely on myself', he ends his story. He pours himself another cup of coffee and leafs through his positive data log.

Not just believing but feeling

What are the signs that things are going in the right direction as far as your self-esteem and confidence are concerned? For instance, do you think about yourself in a positive light more often, do you praise yourself on a regular basis, and are you satisfied with what you do? You may consider your positive qualities and mention them sometimes in conversation with others, and you're probably less reluctant now to accept praise from others. You are more assertive, make fewer demands on yourself, and enjoy small things more.

Behaviour, thoughts, and feelings do not change at the same rate. As a consequence, you might not yet fully believe in the positive statement that you formulated in Chapter 2, even though you have written in your positive data log on a daily basis. You believe it in your head, but might not feel it yet. Maybe you ask yourself whether things will ever be okay, or whether you are a hopeless case. If you are disappointed because you feel you're not quite there yet, there is no reason to lose hope. Like the tortoise and the hare, feelings often lag behind behaviour and thoughts. If you maintain your new positive behaviour, you will come to feel it too.

'A tortoise', Emma thinks, 'that's an apt comparison. Will my feelings ever catch up?' She has done her best to write in her positive data log frequently, thinking up and recording qualities for her positive qualities list regularly too. She has had negative experiences as well, as she was sometimes sad and couldn't seem to raise her mood. But after just a week of feeling sad, she was back on her feet again.

She has also tried out different behaviours. 'The Jack project was a success', she tells Geri. 'I don't let him annoy me any more, even if he is blunt.' She is proud of that and can now even sympathize with Jack. He is quite funny, and sometimes he is right. And what about her second project? 'Not entering through the back, but through the front door' is what she has called it. It encompasses a lot: presenting herself in a positive light, being open about herself, taking the initiative. Very carefully, she has started experimenting and even went to her secondary school reunion and met an old friend there. 'I told her about my life without painting a rosy picture', she wrote in her positive data log, and 'I suggested we meet again.'

Sometimes she feels that she is okay – she not only thinks so, she actually feels it. It would be great if that feeling were always with her, without any interruptions and no downsides! 'Patience is a virtue', Geri tells her, 'do you remember that old saying?'

A maintenance plan

The habit of running yourself into the ground belongs to the past and has been replaced by a greater focus on your strengths. But you are not yet entirely 'cured': your negative core belief has been with you for a very long time and it will not give up easily. However, you have seen that your new approach has favourable effects on your daily life – and there is no greater motivation to continue. If you persist, the result will be even better. Your mood will improve further and you will feel stronger and less vulnerable. You can develop and grow.

In Exercise 9.2, you will complete the Rosenberg Self-Esteem Scale again. Look at the results to see how your self-esteem has fared. In Exercise 9.3, you will rate the credibility of your positive core belief for the last time.

Then you will think about a maintenance plan in Exercise 9.4. How do you maintain what you have learned? Think which exercises helped you most, whether it be the positive data log, the one-minute exercise or the positive story. Or was it paying attention to not putting yourself down, listening to criticism, getting rid of dos and don'ts or the minimum programme? Only you can judge what is best to maintain and build on of what you have learned. You can also decide whether you still need your buddy, whether you might need them as back-up for the future.

'I am afraid to let go of the positive data log', thinks Emma, 'but I do want to stop. I will keep making the one-minute lists.' When she is at Geri's for a week to relax, she goes through the entire positive data log once more and decides to highlight several things from it. She writes them down on little cards and adds a little drawing to each of them. 'I can get mad. I can also keep it in' she writes on the first card. On the second she writes 'I have seen a lot of the world'. Then 'I can enjoy a good movie' on the third and 'I got a positive assessment' on the fourth. She continues with all kinds of things. Geri gives her a beautiful little box. 'For your bedside table', she says.

What if your low self-esteem returns?

Unfortunately, low self-esteem can sometimes return. What is stored in your memory remains stored, so somewhere in the archive there is a box full of negative information. These are painful memories that belong to a period when you were unhappy. Your negative core belief may crop up from time to time and throw you off balance. Nothing to worry about, this is entirely normal.

Certain situations are quite risky:

- *Low or negative mood*. If you are low, negative thoughts and memories present themselves more easily, so you will enter the danger zone.
- *Sensitive subjects*. Rejection or criticism can be a danger. You can deal with mild criticism better now and don't lie awake at night because not everybody likes you, but strong criticism or rejection can hit hard.
- *Tension or stress*. When unpleasant things happen to you, such as the death of a family member, it makes you less stable. If you are unbalanced, old concerns emerge and before you know it, you start thinking negative thoughts about yourself and it is as though nothing ever changed.
- *Big changes in your life*. Even pleasant changes or changes you have chosen for yourself can make you feel less stable. Moving in with a partner, having a baby, moving house or starting a new job can unbalance you. The risk is even greater, of course, if the changes are unpleasant.

There isn't always a clear explanation for a setback. It can happen to anyone. As a back up, think of the measures you can take if you are confronted once more by your old negative core belief. Preparation is key! You will finish this programme by making a contingency plan in Exercise 9.5.

Not everyone is pleased with the fact that Bryony takes more care of herself and less of others. 'My, you have become hard', her mother complained and her aunts have expressed some concern also. Does she maybe have a boyfriend? Only Aunt Jean supports Bryony, saying: 'It is about time you led your own life. You're 32 now, girl. You have a busy job and your own house that take up enough of your time already. Your brother can take care of himself, and your parents too. You are in the prime of your life and now's the time to enjoy it. Go out, meet a man, live!'

'That is easier said than done', thinks Bryony. She has felt better lately, because she no longer runs from pillar to post to please everyone, but her family's criticism hits her hard. Is she too selfish after all? Has she overdone it? Maybe. Is it really so bad to help someone else every now and then? Otherwise, I'd only be watching TV … It keeps worrying her. Perfect time to talk to Bibi …

No worries

Re-experiencing low self-esteem is part of the changing process. There is no reason to panic – just wait a while and see whether your confidence does return. What left of its own accord may come up of its own accord too. But don't let yourself be overwhelmed by the old negative conviction about yourself.

If feeling more confident does not happen spontaneously, do not fool yourself into thinking you are a hopeless case, even though it is easy to think that way when you doubt yourself. Get your contingency plan out and try to do what it says there. Continue doing what you have become used to doing. You can ask your buddy for help, although if you know the risky situation and know what to do when low self-esteem crops back up, you might be able to deal with it on your own.

Michael's contingency plan:
New people are a risk for me, especially at work. When I start worrying about what others think of me and I get the feeling I could be 'found out' at any moment, things are going in the wrong direction. I start acting over-friendly but end up hating myself.

Measures: I had better keep my positive data log again for a while and read my positive qualities list. I should be courageous and keep trying to express my opinions.

It is even more important to register when things are going well. Note the situations in which you manage to maintain your confidence and pay attention to how you react differently. Praise yourself for this and the confidence to conquer your troubles will grow.

Exercises

Exercise 9.1: Writing a positive story about yourself

A healthy level of confidence and self-esteem is based on a rich, balanced and mainly positive view of yourself. It consists of several layers: concrete behaviour, good qualities and, finally, a general notion of yourself as 'good', 'okay', 'worthwhile'– a lovely conclusion.

- *Time to allow: 90 minutes*
- *How to go about it*

  - ✓ Pick a title for your story.
  - ✓ Write a story about yourself in which you make clear what makes you a worthwhile person. Name qualities and how they are visible in what you do and say. Give concrete examples.
  - ✓ A weak point may be mentioned, but should not become dominant.
  - ✓ Let a buddy or significant others read it.

My positive story

Title : ....

....

....

Exercise 9.2: Measuring your self-esteem again

To measure the change in your self-esteem and confidence, complete the Rosenberg Self-Esteem Scale again.

- *Time to allow: 10 minutes*
- *How to go about it*

✔ Read the list of statements.
✔ For each statement, indicate to what degree you agree with it by circling a number in one of columns 2–5.
✔ Calculate your total score by summing the numbers you have circled.
✔ Compare your score with that in **Exercise 2.1 (page 38)**.

	Strongly agree	Agree	Disagree	Strongly disagree
On the whole, I am satisfied with myself	3	2	1	0
At times I think I am no good at all	0	1	2	3
I feel that I have a number of good qualities	3	2	1	0
I am able to do things as well as most other people	3	2	1	0
I feel I do not have much to be proud of	0	1	2	3
I certainly feel useless at times	0	1	2	3
I feel that I am a person of worth, at least on an equal plane with others	3	2	1	0
I wish I could have more respect for myself	0	1	2	3
All in all, I am inclined to feel that I am a failure	0	1	2	3
I take a positive attitude towards myself	3	2	1	0

Total score: ...

The higher your total score, the more confident you are. A score below 18 indicates low self-esteem, while a score below 15 indicates very low self-esteem. A score of 21 or over indicates average or above-average self-esteem.

Exercise 9.3: Rating the credibility of your new core belief
You have tracked your development by reflecting on the credibility of your new positive core belief at the end of each chapter. Now you will do so for the last time.

* *Time to allow: 2 minutes*
* *How to go about it*

   ✓ Copy the positive statement from **Exercise 2.2 (page 39)**.
   ✓ Indicate with a cross how convinced you are of your new core belief.
   ✓ Leaf through the book and note how the credibility has changed over time.
   ✓ If you like, you can make a graph of the scores.

My new positive core belief:
....

Date:
Credibility:

:—:—:—:—:—:—:—:—:—:—:

0   10   20   30   40   50   60   70   80   90   100

0 = not at all credible   100 = highly credible

Exercise 9.4: Thinking about what comes next
Your self-esteem is now healthier, but its foundations still need strengthening. That is why you need to maintain what you have learned.

- *Time to allow: 30 minutes*
- *How to go about it*

    ✓ Note down which exercises helped you most.
    ✓ Pick one or two of them.

My maintenance plan

The following exercises helped me a great deal:

....
....
....
....

In the future I will concentrate on:

....
....

Exercise 9.5: Making a contingency plan

You could wait for a setback and then try to win back all the terrain you lost, but it will take a great deal of effort. Instead, you could prepare a back-up plan beforehand for when things are not going too well.

- *Time to allow: 45 minutes*
- *How to go about it*

    ✓ Identify possible difficult subjects and risky situations.
    ✓ Determine what the first signs of a setback are. Which thoughts enter your mind when your negative view of yourself gains ground again? And which feelings and behaviour?
    ✓ Think of measures you can take: What can you do? Are there any helpful thoughts you can come up with?

My contingency plan

....
....
....
....
....

Measures:

....
....

Further reading

Beck, A.T. and Freeman, A. (1994) *Cognitive Therapy of Personality Disorders.* New York: Guilford Press.

Beck, J.S. (2011) *Cognitive Therapy: Basics and Beyond.* New York: Guilford Press.

Brewin, C.R. (2006) Understanding Cognitive Behaviour Therapy: A Retrieval Competition Account, *Behaviour Research and Therapy,* 44, 765–84.

Calkin, A.B. (2000) *A Minute a Day Makes Good Feelings Grow: Behavior in Everyday Life.* Beverly, MA: Cambridge Center for Behavioral Studies [www.behavior.org].

Fennell, M. (2011) *Boost Your Confidence: Improving Self-Esteem Step-By-Step.* London: Robinson.

Fennell, M. and Brosan, L. (2011) *An Introduction to Improving Your Self-Esteem.* London: Robinson.

Korrelboom, K., Maarsingh, M. and Huijbrechts, I. (2012) Competitive Memory Training (COMET) for Treating Low Self-Esteem in Patients with Depressive Disorders: A Randomized Clinical Trial, *Depression and Anxiety,* 77, 974–80.

Mann, M., Hosman, C.M.H., Schaalma, H.P. and de Vries, N.K. (2004) Self-Esteem in a Broad-Spectrum Approach for Mental Health Promotion, *Health Education Research,* 19, 357–72.

McKay, M. and Fanning, P. (2000) *Self-Esteem: A Proven Program of Cognitive Techniques for Assessing, Improving and Maintaining Your Self-Esteem.* Oakland, CA: New Harbinger Publications.

McLeod, A.K. and Moore, R. (2000) Positive Thinking Revisited: Positive Cognitions, Well-Being and Mental Health, *Clinical Psychology and Psychotherapy,* 7, 1–10.

Padesky, C. (1994) Schema Change Processes in Cognitive Therapy, *Clinical Psychology and Psychotherapy,* 1, 267–78.

STOP WORRYING
Get Your Life Back on Track with CBT

Ad Kerkhof

ISBN: 9780335242528 (Paperback)
eBook: 9780335242535
2010

This practical book will give you insight into the content, nature and seriousness of your worrying.

Key features:

- Supports and offers advice to worriers
- Contains Cognitive Behavioural Therapy exercises
- Provides guidance for professionals

www.openup.co.uk

 OPEN UNIVERSITY PRESS
McGraw - Hill Education

A BEGINNER'S GUIDE TO MINDFULNESS
Live in the moment

Bohlmeijer and Hulsbergen

ISBN: 9780335247356 (Paperback)
eBook: 9780335247363
2013

This practical book will help you to experience greater freedom and quality in your life and teach you how to cope with stressful situations.

Combining mindfulness and Acceptance and Commitment Therapy (ACT) exercises in an accessible 9-week programme, Bohlmeijer and Hulsbergen show you how to observe your thoughts without judgement and connect with the 'here and now' in your life.

www.openup.co.uk

OPEN UNIVERSITY PRESS
McGraw - Hill Education